Smart Robotics with LEGO MINDSTORMS Robot Inventor

Learn to play with the LEGO MINDSTORMS Robot Inventor kit and build creative robots

Aaron Maurer

BIRMINGHAM—MUMBAI

Smart Robotics with LEGO MINDSTORMS Robot Inventor

Commissioning Editor: Wilson D'souza
Publishing Product Manager: Sankalp Khattri
Senior Editor: Arun Nadar
Content Development Editor: Mrudgandha Kulkarni
Technical Editor: Nithik Cheruvakodan
Copy Editor: Safis Editing
Project Coordinator: Shagun Saini
Proofreader: Safis Editing
Indexer: Priyanka Dhadke
Production Designer: Alishon Mendonca

First published: April 2021
Production reference: 1070521

Published by Packt Publishing Ltd.
Livery Place
35 Livery Street
Birmingham
B3 2PB, UK.

ISBN 978-1-80056-840-2

www.packt.com

Contributors

About the author

Aaron Maurer, also known as **Coffeechug**, is the STEM lead for 21 school districts in Iowa, helping to expand STEM, computer science, makerspace, and purposeful play into K-12 classrooms. Aaron was also a **FIRST** (**For Inspiration and Recognition of Science and Technology**) LEGO League coach for 8 years with much success, working with phenomenal kids.

He has a **master's degree in secondary education**. Aaron is also a member of NCCE, LEGO Education Master Educator, OBS Digital Innovator and All-Star, PITSCO TAG, Microsoft Innovative Educator Expert and Fellow, Minecraft Global Mentor, and micro:bit champion.

Finally, Aaron was a finalist for the **Iowa Teacher of the Year** award in 2014.

You can find more of his work at www.coffeeforthebrain.com.

About the reviewer

Khushboo Samkaria (Rana) lives in India with her husband, Vivek, and son, Agastya. She is a certified **LEGO Serious Play (LSP)** practitioner with more than 8 years of experience working globally with LEGO education partners and organizing **FIRST (For Inspiration and Recognition of Science and Technology)** programs. She is devoted to the mission of helping young innovators to understand the real world using an interdisciplinary approach, **STEM (Science, Technology, Engineering, Math)**, and has interacted with more than 100,000 kids and adults globally since 2011. Currently, she works with various organizations to help them tap their unused knowledge and ideas using the LSP approach so that they can succeed in this period of intense change, such as the COVID-19 pandemic.

Packt is searching for authors like you

If you're interested in becoming an author for Packt, please visit authors. packtpub.com and apply today. We have worked with thousands of developers and tech professionals, just like you, to help them share their insight with the global tech community. You can make a general application, apply for a specific hot topic that we are recruiting an author for, or submit your own idea.

Table of Contents

4
Building a LEGO Guitar

5
Building a Scorpion

6

Building a Solid Sumobot

7

Building a Dragster

8

Building an Egg and Ornament Decorator

9

Creating Plankton from SpongeBob SquarePants – Part 1

10

Creating Plankton from SpongeBob SquarePants – Part 2

Other Books You May Enjoy

Index

Preface

Welcome to this book. I am so excited to have the opportunity to share with you a passion of mine as an educator who has hands-on experience with LEGO, transforming learning and engagement with students, a parent who has spent countless hours building and creating stories with my kids, an **Adult Fan of LEGO (AFOL)** with my own LEGO collection to fulfill my hobby, and, of course, just someone who loves the energy of the LEGO community and the continuous positive sharing of remarkable ideas.

I have one major goal with this book: I want this book to be a permission slip for you to build and make. Sometimes when we read books such as these, we build as suggested in the book and that is the extent of the creative process. Being an educator who has spent time in elementary and middle schools, I have learned that not providing the answer is the true facilitator of creativity. What I have created is a series of builds not only for you to explore the new LEGO Robot Inventor Kit but also the world of smart robots that impact our daily lives.

So, each chapter will explore a smart robot concept to explore along with a model robot to build. However, each build has been designed for you to add your own touch. You will see suggestions and ideas to apply the learning of the chapter into new layers of building. I hope you love the freedom to take the ideas and build your own version.

With this permission slip, I cannot wait to see what you create. Make sure you share!

Here we go. Let's go explore the new LEGO MINDSTORMS Robot Inventor Kit that is now available.

Who this book is for

The audience of this book is robot enthusiasts, LEGO lovers, hobbyists of tinkering, educators, students, and anyone who is looking to learn about the new LEGO Robot Inventor Kit. The book is designed to go beyond basic builds to intermediate and advanced builds, but keeping it open enough to explore how to add personal flare to the builds and code.

Anyone can complete these builds regardless of background. If you have a growth mindset and love learning, then that is all you need to be successful with the robots in this book.

What this book covers

Chapter 1, History of MINDSTORMS, focuses on a very brief and quick history of the LEGO MINDSTORMS timeline. This chapter serves as information and context for this new **MINDSTORMS Robot Inventor Kit 51515.** It provides a backdrop of how we have arrived at this new kit.

Chapter 2, Getting Started with the Robot Inventor Kit, is focused on getting familiar with the various parts and components available in the LEGO Robot Inventor Kit and finishes with a small build to explore the basics of the kit.

Chapter 3, Building an Industrial Robot Claw, is focused on how the user can use different components available in the Robot Inventor Kit to build a working model of a robotic arm.

Chapter 4, Building a LEGO Guitar, is focused on combining robotics and music by using the Robot Inventor Kit to make a guitar that is playable and codable to our unique needs and musical tastes.

Chapter 5, Building a Scorpion, is focused on how to build a scorpion robot designed around the famous features of this creature. In particular, you will be building the stinger and a body style similar to a scorpion along with some additional features that the kit provides.

Chapter 6, Building a Solid Sumobot, is focused on how to build a sumobot that will endure battle in a sumo arena while utilizing sensors to be more effective in a strategy designed for success.

Chapter 7, Building a Dragster, is focused on how to build a dragster to see how it turns out in terms of speed and design.

Chapter 8, Building an Egg and Ornament Decorator, is focused on building a robot that will spin around objects such as eggs or ornaments for you to be able to design patterns using markers and other art materials.

Chapter 9, Creating Plankton from SpongeBob SquarePants Part 1, is focused on building the main component of Plankton for the robot to showcase animatronics.

Chapter 10, Creating Plankton from SpongeBob SquarePants Part 2, is focused on building the rest of Plankton by adding the final details to the build and programming the robot to be interactive.

To get the most out of this book

To be successful and get the most out of this book, you will need the following materials and software:

Software/hardware covered in the book	OS requirements
The LEGO MINDSTORMS Robot Inventor software	Windows, Mac, iOS, Android, or Fire OS
LEGO MINDSTORMS Robot Inventor Kit #51515	

If you are using the digital version of this book, we advise you to type the code yourself or access the code via the GitHub repository (link available in the next section). Doing so will help you avoid any potential errors related to the copying and pasting of code. The programming software can be used on computers and/or tablets/phone. You may want to explore and experiment with both platforms to find out what you prefer.

Download the example code files

You can download the example code files for this book from GitHub at `https://github.com/PacktPublishing/Smart-Robotics-with-LEGO-MINDSTORMS-Robot-Inventor/`. In case there's an update to the code, it will be updated on the existing GitHub repository.

We also have other code bundles from our rich catalog of books and videos available at `https://github.com/PacktPublishing/`. Check them out!

Code in Action

Code in Action videos for this book can be viewed at `http://bit.ly/2Ovna4w`.

Download the color images

We also provide a PDF file that has color images of the screenshots/diagrams used in this book. You can download it here: `http://www.packtpub.com/sites/default/files/downloads/9781800568402_ColorImages.pdf`.

Conventions used

There are a number of text conventions used throughout this book.

`Code in text`: Indicates code words in text, database table names, folder names, filenames, file extensions, pathnames, dummy URLs, user input, and Twitter handles. Here is an example: "You will drop in another **Set Action** block with the condition of 4 to activate that code sequence in our main program."

Bold: Indicates a new term, an important word, or words that you see onscreen. For example, words in menus or dialog boxes appear in the text like this. Here is an example: "Insert another **If** block nested in the **Forever** block and underneath our first **If** block."

> **Tips or important notes**
> Appear like this.

Get in touch

Feedback from our readers is always welcome.

General feedback: If you have questions about any aspect of this book, mention the book title in the subject of your message and email us at `customercare@packtpub.com`.

Errata: Although we have taken every care to ensure the accuracy of our content, mistakes do happen. If you have found a mistake in this book, we would be grateful if you would report this to us. Please visit `www.packtpub.com/support/errata`, selecting your book, clicking on the Errata Submission Form link, and entering the details.

Piracy: If you come across any illegal copies of our works in any form on the Internet, we would be grateful if you would provide us with the location address or website name. Please contact us at `copyright@packt.com` with a link to the material.

If you are interested in becoming an author: If there is a topic that you have expertise in and you are interested in either writing or contributing to a book, please visit `authors.packtpub.com`.

Reviews

Please leave a review. Once you have read and used this book, why not leave a review on the site that you purchased it from? Potential readers can then see and use your unbiased opinion to make purchase decisions, we at Packt can understand what you think about our products, and our authors can see your feedback on their book. Thank you!

For more information about Packt, please visit `packt.com`.

1
History of Mindstorms

This chapter is going to focus on a very brief and quick history of the LEGO Mindstorms timeline. This chapter serves as information and context for the new **Mindstorms Robot Inventor Kit 51515**. It will provide a backdrop of how we have arrived at this new kit.

It is hard to believe that LEGO has been in the robotics environment for over 20 years. Today the educational and consumer world is saturated with robots. We see them everywhere, from toys to day-to-day life products, and all over the industrial and economic world.

Back in 1998, LEGO released **Lego Mindstorms: The Robotics Invention System**. There were some other products created by LEGO prior to this kit, but for all intents and purposes, we are going to focus on this first RCX Mindstorms kit, 9719, as the kicking-off point for our quick journey through the robotic systems over time.

The reason we are going to do a quick dive into the incredible history of LEGO Mindstorms is to realize how far technology has progressed and to pave the way for understanding what this new kit is providing us. I think it is easy to overlook how accessible some of this incredible technology has become to help us to learn and bring our ideas to life.

For the sake of brevity, we are only going to focus on the Mindstorms line. Please realize that there are so many other incredible products, such as the **WeDo**, **STEAM Park**, **Coding Express**, and **Boost** to name a few. There are even robot kits that were designed by LEGO prior to the RCX.

Finally, this chapter is not going to explore all the coding platforms and languages because that can get quite lengthy and complicated. If you are interested in learning more about coding platforms, then please explore the chart maintained by *David Lechner* and *Seshan Brothers* as it is the best reference of all that is possible; it can be accessed from the *Further reference* section at the end of this chapter.

In this chapter, we're going to cover the following main topics:

- 1998 – LEGO Mindstorms: The Robotics Invention System (RCX)
- 2006 – LEGO Mindstorms NXT
- 2013 – LEGO Mindstorms EV3
- 2020 – LEGO SPIKE Prime
- 2020 – LEGO Mindstorms Robot Inventor Kit

Technical requirements

For this chapter, there are no technical requirements.

1998 – LEGO Mindstorms: The Robotics Invention System (RCX)

If we start several years prior to 1998 and look back to 1982, LEGO had a new product line called **Technic** (have you heard of it?). A few years into this new line of products, LEGO began to work with *Seymour Papert* (one of my educational heroes) to create programmable LEGO. *Papert* even has a book called *Mindstorms* (ironic?). One of Papert's colleagues, named *Mitch Resnick* (from *MIT Lifelong Kindergarten*), who I have had the pleasure of meeting, presented a prototype to LEGO in Billund and things started to take shape.

Fast forward to 1998, when LEGO released the **Robot Command eXplorer** (**RCX**):

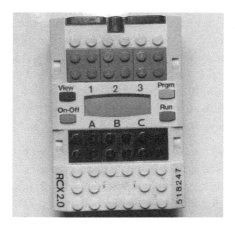

Figure 1.1 – RCX 2.00 brick hub

You'll know this brick as the yellow brick that started a journey unlike any other – a powerful programming device with 32 KB of RAM with no USB (not available to the public until September 1998), no Wi-Fi (cell phones were just emerging with games such as **Snake**), or anything we would expect today. It used a LEGO IR tower to send code from the computer to the RCX brick. If you still have Windows 98, ME, or XP, you could still boot up and code today.

2006 – LEGO Mindstorms NXT

Cue the fond memories of the gray and orange NXT robotics kit. Heading back in time, I vividly remember hosting my first robotics summer camp for students when I found out I had access to seven of these kits. This was also the time when I first dipped my toe into the FIRST LEGO League:

Figure 1.2 – LEGO Mindstorms NXT brick

In 2006, LEGO updated the robot line with the NXT. I am sure many of you remember, recognize, or have fond memories of using the NXT. There were two versions of this kit, retail (8527) and educational (9797). Additionally, the kits had an upgrade to NXT 2.0 (8547). More importantly, the programming interface was LabVIEW, which is what many of us grew to love with the NXT and EV3. It was also with this robotic kit that there started to be a huge list of various programming languages made available by third parties if you did not want to use block-based coding.

In 2009, LEGO upgraded this kit with an NXT 2.0 (8547) that provided some updates with a new color sensor that was available in the retail version of this product. This brick allowed the user to program images and edit sounds. Additionally, it had four buttons to navigate on the brick. What I loved most about this kit was that there was a sound sensor that was provided in the education kit (9797). You could activate the robot based on sound. While this sensor went away in future kits, I find it fascinating that as we explore smart robots in this book, LEGO was ahead of its time as almost all of us now have an Alexa, Siri, or Cortana device that is activated by sound and voice.

In terms of the retail kits, the color sensor found in NXT 2.0 replaced the light sensor found in NXT 1.0 in the retail kit.

2013 – LEGO Mindstorms EV3

We now enter the era of LEGO robotics when almost everyone reading this book spent more hours than they care to admit building, programming, and designing robots using the LEGO EV3. Whether you build as a hobby as a child or **Adult Fan of LEGO (AFOL)**, enter competitions such as **FIRST LEGO League**, teach in education settings, or simply just love using LEGO to bring ideas to life, we can all agree that the **EV3** is a rather robust robotic kit that allows the builder to accomplish just about anything:

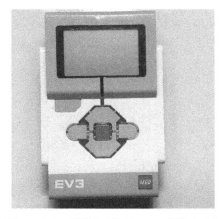

Figure 1.3 – LEGO Mindstorms EV3 brick

Because this kit has been around for a while, and also due to its popularity, there are so many third-party sensors and add-ons available that the sky is truly the limit when it comes to designing ideas.

Just like the NXT, LEGO released two versions of this kit. There was the retail version and the educational version. Again, builders used a version of **LabVIEW** to program, but recently you could also program this brick in Python to really push its capability. As technology and accessibility have improved, you could also do all the programming online using tools such as **MakeCode**, providing new pathways for people to get involved in programming.

There were some subtle differences between the two kits, but enough to make it worth mentioning:

- **Retail**: Had a total of 601 pieces and included two large motors, one medium motor, one touch sensor, one color sensor, one infrared sensor, and one remote control
- **Education**: Had a total of 541 pieces and included one EV3 programmable brick, two large motors, one medium motor, two touch sensors, one color sensor, one gyroscopic sensor, and one ultrasonic sensor

Additionally, the education version also had an expansion kit (45560), which provided some new elements not seen before and bonus builds to really help engage students in new ways of building and programming.

The changes and upgrades in elements are interesting to follow as technology continues to change in our world all around us. Perhaps the most important feature to take note of as these kits continued to be upgraded is the fact that while the EV3 had a USB cable and Bluetooth like the NXT, it always allowed for Wi-Fi, bringing more opportunities to builders.

Regardless of the kit that you used, this has been our world. Builders have done some incredible things with these kits that really helped to transform LEGO from a toy to a legit product of engineering and coding marvel.

2020 – LEGO SPIKE Prime

2020 ended up being a big year for LEGO. This kit was originally slated for release in August 2019, but it did not actually hit the market until January 2020. This is a fascinating kit to explore because it marked a shift to a new era of STEM, robotics, and marketing for the LEGO audience:

Figure 1.4 – LEGO SPIKE Prime brick

This kit is a LEGO Education product, but it is available on the main LEGO site. We see a transition away from making two kits, one retail and one education. Instead, it is available to all, which is a smart move as the boundaries of learning have become so intertwined, with virtual learning, homeschool, after-school events, and regular school.

This kit is designed for an upper elementary and middle school audience (grades 6–8). The builder will notice some changes from previous kits. First, the color scheme is brighter and more alive compared to the whites, grays, and blacks of the previous kits. There are a host of new elements that make building so much nicer.

Another big change is the move away from LabVIEW to a Scratch-based programming interface. Depending on who you are and your previous experience using LabVIEW, you'll either love or dislike this move. However, moving forward, having all the robot kits using one interface will make the product line much nicer to work with and interact with various kits.

One big difference between this kit and previous kits is the connectors. The connectors are a much thinner wire. While this will help with programming and building, it does mean that all of our previous sensors and motors are not compatible with these new kits. By the time this book is published, I am sure a third-party company will have devised an adapter, but in the meantime, we will have to use the new elements and only use the wires provided instead of finding the length that we desire.

The LEGO SPIKE Prime kit also has an expansion kit (45680) that contains over 600 more elements to build new projects and robots and to help make the robot competitive in events such as FLL.

Finally, SPIKE Prime contains many lessons, build guides, and more for parents and teachers to get started with their students/children with building on the LEGO Education website as well as in the software. This has always been a strong point of LEGO products, providing support and resources to go along with an amazing product. Even adults will find these useful to get used to the new coding interface that is Scratch-based versus LabVIEW.

It should also be noted that the LEGO SPIKE Prime is not technically in the official Mindstorms progression of robotic kits by LEGO, but it is included as it is so close to the new Inventor Kit and marks a shift in the new brick structure for LEGO. As we explore in *Chapter 2*, *Getting Started and Understanding the Robot Inventor Kit*, you will see many similarities between the SPIKE Prime and Robot Inventor, which is why this kit is included in this history of Mindstorms.

With this new design of the brick, you can program the LED matrix on the Intelligent Hub. It is worth noting that in previous models of the bricks, you could program the screen with graphics, words, and data. It is referred to as *programmable LED* due to the fact that the design approach to the screen has changed, using a *4x5* LED array.

2020 – LEGO Mindstorms Robot Inventor Kit

All of this history brings us to the latest LEGO robotics kit, the LEGO Mindstorms Robot Inventor Kit (51515). Let's take a look at what we know about this kit.

First, just to be clear, this is the kit that is designed to be the new robot in the Mindstorms product line. The SPIKE Prime is designed for a specific age and this kit is the new version of the Mindstorms. You will notice on the LEGO site that EV3 is now marked as retiring soon.

There are many similar features that compare to the SPIKE Prime. First, the hub is the same, with a rechargeable hub. The hub works with an app to allow Bluetooth programming and building. The difference between the brick hubs is simply the color scheme. The Robot Inventor brick has a teal color while the SPIKE Prime has a yellow color:

Figure 1.5 – LEGO Mindstorms Robot Inventor Hub

We will explore in greater detail the new parts, elements, coding, platforms, and more in the next chapter, where we will take a deeper dive into the contents of the kit. That is the reason you are reading this book, so be prepared to learn about the kit through hands-on experience.

Summary

As we took a trip down memory lane, we witnessed how LEGO has evolved their products as technology, costs, and opportunities present themselves. It is crazy to think that this work has been going on since the 90s. Depending on your experience and when you first entered the Mindstorms world, we all have a favorite product. Whether you are a die-hard NXT fan, still hanging on to the glory of EV3, or excited about the new possibilities of the Robot Inventor Kit, we are fortunate to have such cool robotics to bring the ideas in our minds to life.

Change is always happening and sometimes we like change and sometimes we don't. As our world changes daily, so do the opportunities we have to build, program, and play. This latest kit by LEGO is going to provide us with so many wonderful opportunities to bring the ideas in our heads into the real world. Let's take a closer look at the new kit and explore the new elements included in the kit, along with some of the new programming features, so we can begin to understand the platform to design some smart robots.

In the next chapter, we will dive into the new parts, elements, coding apps, and more that come with the Mindstorms Robot Inventor Kit.

Further reference

- This link will take you to a spreadsheet displaying all the possible programming languages allowed in FIRST LEGO League and the programming languages not allowed, to help you explore all the possibilities of coding: `https://docs.google.com/spreadsheets/d/1OxyXEIB5pHzOSpAuOKY_2XeK1Uomv7lzHLVG1ZKLFH8/edit#gid=0`.

2
Getting Started with the Robot Inventor Kit

Let's get started with exploring the kit. We have over 900 elements to build robots, upgraded sensors, a new Intelligent Hub compared to previous versions, and new programming platforms to bring our robots to life and control:

Figure 2.1 – The front of the box when you get your hands on this amazing kit

To begin with, we are going to examine what the new elements in this kit are for us to build within our designs, how the sensors have changed, and the new Intelligent Hub. As we explore, we will take a closer look at some excellent features of this kit to start learning more about this LEGO Mindstorms product.

Finally, we will do some exploration of the new programming interface and how we use code to bring our ideas to life. The end goal of this chapter is to make sure you understand all the possibilities and to build a foundation of basic knowledge of the kit to begin to build some of the exciting ideas to follow in the upcoming chapters. This would also be a perfect time to build some or all of the five robots that come with the software to see how everything works and operates. There is not any specific building in this chapter, but it serves as an understanding of what can be achieved with the parts.

In this chapter, we're going to cover the following main topics:

- Overview of the kit
- The Intelligent Hub
- New elements
- Sensors
- Programming
- Basic projects to learn more

Technical requirements

One of the creative constraints when designing the builds in this book is to only use the parts, sensors, and elements contained in the kit. There will not be any additional parts needed to complete any of these builds. You will need LEGO Mindstorms Robot Inventor Kit 51515.

For software, you will need to download the LEGO Mindstorms Inventor software on either your computer, phone, or tablet. Please check the site to ensure your hardware is compatible with the software. You can find all hardware compatibility information on the LEGO site at https://www.lego.com/en-us/service/device-guide/mindstorms-robot-inventor.

You can access the code for this chapter here: https://github.com/PacktPublishing/Smart-Robotics-with-LEGO-MINDSTORMS-Robot-Inventor/blob/main/Chapter%202%20Rock%20Paper%20Scissors%20Code.lms.

If you would like a more detailed photo-by-photo build process of the robot, please head here: `https://bit.ly/3eS6Cif`.

Overview of the kit

This kit comes with 949 elements to build, design, and bring your ideas to life. When you open the box, you will find that the inside of the box has outlines to organize your elements. However, I don't think that many will use this grid unless you are crafty and install some cardboard walls to make it usable. Additionally, to have both box pieces on a table occupies a lot of space. While a nice feature, it is better if you use a leftover Mindstorms storage container or any other sorting trays you have sitting around. Or you could be like most people and just dump all the elements and spend time trying to find that one piece.

Coming from the space of education, I miss the plastic tub with sorting trays. The latest tub from SPIKE Prime has two trays that come together, which is super nice. I really wish we had this with this kit.

The kit does not have a manual to build robots, but the software comes with five robot builds to help a builder learn some new build techniques and to get started with building robots. The software provides the builder with the build instructions, then you connect the Intelligent Hub, download the software, test to make sure it works, and then modify to make the build and/or the code to your own style. It is quite nice once you get started with the software to see what it all provides.

Here is what the kit provides:

- One micro USB cable
- One Intelligent Hub
- A sticker sheet
- One base
- 14 bags of building elements
- External sensors (one distance sensor, one color sensor)
- Motors (four small motors)
- A booklet

We will explore these parts in greater detail throughout this chapter to understand them better.

The cables for motors and sensors

One of the biggest changes that the builder will notice right away is the cable connections. If you have not used SPIKE Prime and this is your first transition to the new Intelligent Hub, then you will notice that the cables are different. They are flat and smooth:

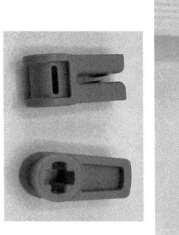

Figure 2.2 – Flat wires and wire clips

The kit comes with clips to help with wire organization and building, which is an excellent new upgrade to the building kits. No more rubber bands and looping cables. These clips are really nice to hide cables and manage them to allow your builds to look much more polished. The downside to these new cables is that these cables, sensors, and motors are no longer compatible with previous kits. If you are like me, then you'll have a lot of NXT and EV3 parts that you love that are no longer compatible with these new features. Another downside at this time is the cables are of fixed length. In previous kits, the cables were separate from the elements, so you had a wide range of wire sizes to fit your build. I am sure it won't be long before third-party companies create extensions, but in terms of the actual kit, all your wire lengths are the same, so plan your builds accordingly.

One other change to the kit from previous models is the lack of a remote. In previous models, you had an IR sensor and remote. In this kit, you use your phone or another Bluetooth-enabled controller. I don't think many will have any issues with this and will be excited to pair their Xbox or PlayStation controllers to their robots. The possibilities with Bluetooth are going to really open up some exciting features.

Let's dive into some specific parts and pieces worth exploring.

The Intelligent Hub

Another upgrade to this kit from previous versions is the size of the Intelligent Hub. The Hub is much smaller, which allows for more unique builds especially when combined with some of the new elements. The bulkiness of the EV3 and NXT is no longer going to be an issue. The way the Intelligent Hub is designed allows the builder to position the Intelligent Hub in a variety of ways to allow more easily building designs:

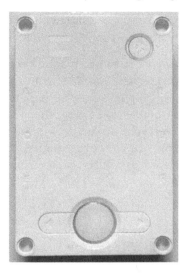

Figure 2.3 – The new Intelligent Hub that comes with the kit

The LED screen is one of the most noticeable changes to the Intelligent Hub. In previous models, we had a screen where the programmer could program on the Intelligent Hub and have various elements of text, data, and graphical images displayed on the screen. On this Intelligent Hub, we are given a 5x5 LED screen. The days of programming on the Intelligent Hub are gone with this new design. However, keep in mind that it is now so much easier to get your programs to the Intelligent Hub. Once your Intelligent Hub is paired to your software, you can make changes instantly, so this feature is no longer needed.

The new Intelligent Hub has an LED design that reminds me of my 8-bit glory days of playing Tetris. These LED blocks allow you to gather some basic data on your sensors, then switch programs, and you are able to write out words that scroll across the screen. Additionally, you use the arrow buttons to scroll through your programs and you are able to store 10 programs.

Using the large button on the Intelligent Hub, you can gather some quick data and test your sensors and motors by plugging them in and gaining some quick information.

The Intelligent Hub has the gyro sensor built in. In the EV3, the gyro was a sensor we had to attach much like the touch, color, and ultrasonic sensors. This is a nice touch to the Intelligent Hub especially now that the Intelligent Hub has been reduced from eight ports to six. While at first you might be sad to only have six ports, remember this could prove to be helpful as these six ports can be both input and output. Looking back at the EV3, it had four ports for motors and four ports for sensors. The new Intelligent Hub allows the user to use any port for any motor or sensor. If you have been using EV3 for as long as I have, then you'll realize that this means you could potentially have six motors running off the hub or six sensors, whereas in the previous models, we were limited to four or fewer.

The Intelligent Hub also contains an accelerometer, an internal speaker, and a rechargeable lithium-ion battery. These functions expand the Intelligent Hub to allow the builder to do some really exciting projects. We will explore some of these features later, but it is a great reminder that the Intelligent Hub now serves as more than just the brains of the operation. It has several new features to expand what we can do with our robots without having to use ports. For example, you can now run your program tethered to your device or connect via Bluetooth for a wireless experience, as well as using your phone/tablet as a controller.

Elements

Depending on what previous LEGO Mindstorms kits you have used in the past and whether you have any experience with SPIKE Prime or some Power-Up kits, these elements might look familiar.

For the sake of exploring the kit, I would like to highlight a few key elements that I believe are great to have that the previous EV3 kit did not provide.

A quick note about the elements is that while many of the pieces are not necessarily new, there are several that come in the kit that are in a very nice-looking teal color. This will be a huge bonus for many builders looking to expand and coordinate their builds to have a more polished look. Teal is a great color choice, allowing the build designs to look really sharp. It is a great added color compared to the white, gray, and black of EV3 while not feeling too colorful like the SPIKE Prime. I like the colors of both kits, but I *really* like having choices in how my robots look.

Let's examine a few specific elements that come in the kit that are worth exploring a bit more deeply.

Panel plate

I fell in love with this piece when I purchased the SPIKE Prime kit. That kit provided two of these. The Robot Inventor provides one of these in that wonderful teal color, which is a very beautiful color scheme with this kit:

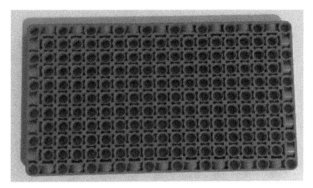

Figure 2.4 – The 11x19x1 panel plate

This plate allows the builder to build right upon it for stationary robots as well as a starting point for other robot builds, such as a vehicle or another mechanism. The possibilities this element provides the builder are huge. It is the piece I wish I always had.

Wheels

The kit provides six of these tires. These tires are great. They are all the same 56 mm size and are all black. They are one piece that is nice compared to the previous wheels. They are easy to clean for smooth driving and having six of these wheels to build with will allow the builder to build some excellent designs:

Figure 2.5 – This is the standard tire that comes with the kit

If you are looking for larger wheels that are built similar to these, there are a pair of larger wheels featured in the SPIKE Prime expansion kit.

Black frames

There are three sizes of these elements that come in the kit. These black frames provide a nice way to build some larger robots and to build more secure structures. You don't realize how much you need these elements until you build with them. Once you have them in your collection, you come to depend on them quite a bit:

Figure 2.6 – The three open frame sizes – from the top, 11x15, 7x11, and 5x7 – that come with the kit

Now that you have explored a few of the larger key elements, let's dive into some specific parts that are included in the kit.

Gear differential

The kit comes with a new gear differential that I know many builders will love. I do not have an extensive history with this aspect of building, but from what I have read and discussed, this piece will prove to be quite useful as builds on vehicles and robots are designed and built:

Figure 2.7 – Gear differential elements

Some of you will love the gear differential, but not everyone builds with these parts. However, there are some parts that almost everyone will love having in the kit. Let's check some of these out.

Mudguards

I love that this kit comes with two mudguard elements. What I love about these elements, and all elements of LEGO, is that while the pieces were designed for a purpose, they can be remixed for all sorts of new ideas. As you explore the kit, consider how you can use pieces in new ways. For example, these elements could prove to be helpful in designing a moving mouth, handles to carry, the frame of a face, and so on:

Figure 2.8 – Mudguards

While these are great pieces, here is another element in the kit that is even cooler!

Projectile launcher

This piece might be my favorite, but as an educator, it would easily be a headache! I know this kit does not come with a touch/force sensor, but the fact that it comes with two of these is great for coming up with new ideas. While there is fun in creating robots that shoot projectiles, such as Blast, which is one of the five builds, these can prove to be helpful in some other build ideas. And who doesn't love to launch projectiles?! This is a great addition to this kit to increase engagement and excitement:

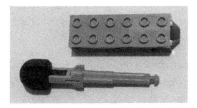

Figure 2.9 – Projectile launchers

Next, let's look at sensors!

Sensors

This kit is limited when it comes to external sensors. In previous kits, the builder was given a variety of sensors to use. Keep in mind that while this kit only provides two external sensors, there are sensors built into the Intelligent Hub. Overall, you are given the following sensors:

- Inbuilt sensors:

  Gyro

  Accelerometer

  Timer

- External sensors:

  Color sensor

  Distance sensor

The Intelligent Hub itself contains an accelerometer and gyroscope, which is great as you can use the data they collect to write some quality code with your robots. Another neat feature of the Intelligent Hub and these sensors are the gesture controls that allow the builder to create code based on tap, free fall, and shake using these sensors:

Figure 2.10 – The distance sensor on the left and the color sensor on the right that come with the kit

There are a few more details worth mentioning. The color sensor has been upgraded compared to previous versions. The color sensor is able to identify a small dose of color to make decisions. The sensor can also detect eight colors. Finally, it can identify these colors in both dark and bright light, which is very helpful. The sensor allows the coder to use color and reflection light.

The distance sensor is relatively similar to previous models except for a few changes. First, it has lights around the eye parts of the sensor that can be activated. The builder can program these lights, which is a cool feature.

The sensor is more accurate than previous models, but the range has been reduced from 250 cm to 200 cm. This will not impact many builders but is worth noting. You can choose distance settings of inches, centimeters, or percent.

Overall, the kit provides the builder with four motors and two sensors along with the sensors built into the Intelligent Hub itself, providing countless opportunities for building and coding.

Motors

This kit provides the builder with four motors. These motors have a top speed of 185 RPM along with a max torque of 18 Ncm. Additionally, the motors have sensors that allow you to gather data on both speed and position when using the app. One thing you will notice is that these medium motors are smaller than the medium motors of previous kits, but are much easier to build within your designs. This is a nice feature to allow the builder to create more fluid and precise builds. The shape also allows for easier builds than previous models where the motors had some unique shapes that could challenge how the builder created their creations:

Figure 2.11 – The design of the medium motors in the kit

The new motors are different from the NXT and EV3 motors. In the previous kits, you were able to put an axle all the way through the motor. These new motors do not allow the builder to do this build. At first, I did not like this, but I realized quickly that it did not prevent any builds from being successful.

One key advantage to these motors is their absolute positioning. This helps with the alignment of motors and to have more precise positioning when using robots that require motors to be synced.

Now that we have a better understanding of the elements of the kit, it is time to explore the software to bring the builds to life.

Hub connection

Using the Mindstorms software, you can adjust the sensor settings by clicking on the sensor icon and adjusting as needed. The following screenshots show how you can use the software to gather data on your motors and sensors and make the necessary adjustments to the needs of your build:

1. In order to access the Hub connection, you will need to open up a new program or any existing program you have already started.

2. In the upper right-hand corner, there is an Intelligent Hub icon that you will click on to open up the interface:

Figure 2.12 – The Hub connection icon in the upper right-hand corner.

You will notice a green dot on the upper right corner of the brick icon which means the Hub is connected. If the color dot is pink then that means your Intelligent Hub is disconnected.

3. You will see this screen that will showcase all the motors and sensors currently plugged in and activated on the Intelligent Hub:

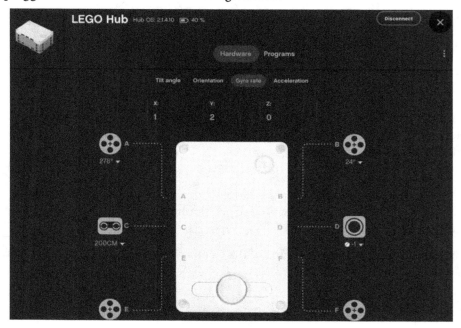

Figure 2.13 – The software interface allowing you to see the data from inputs and outputs

4. Select a motor or sensor and click the white triangle below the icon to choose the various types of data readings that you can use for your projects:

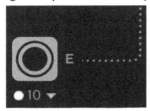

Figure 2.14 – The white triangle next to a data reading opens up a sub-menu of options

5. For the inbuilt sensors, click on the sensor you want to see the information for, and then move your Intelligent Hub around to see the data readings change:

Tilt angle	Orientation	Gyro rate	Acceleration
Yaw:	Pitch:		Roll:
-179	90		0

Figure 2.15 – The four inbuilt sensor data readings for the Intelligent Hub

Now that the Hub connection is done, let's move on to the coding!

Programming

When you boot up the software, you will have the choice to build any of the five robots already loaded up for you to build and use the code provided. Follow the instructions online provided in the software. If you need more information about the software and hardware and details about the kit, then head to https://www.lego.com/en-de/themes/mindstorms/about and you will get what you need from this page.

I find having the software on a computer or laptop for coding is quite helpful because of the larger screen and being able to store programs into my system. It is a good idea to have the software installed on your tablet or phone because these are good for the remote control feature of the software. Explore all the options to find what works best for you as a designer.

To get started, with **version 10.0.3 (713488)**, LEGO updated the software to give you an option to get a quick overview of the sensors and builds and how they work with the Intelligent Hub. If you have any experience with Mindstorms, then you won't necessarily need this, but it is a great addition for those who are new to the Mindstorms robotics systems.

However, this little build and coding activity is a great start to explore much of the content shared in this chapter.

You can access this activity anytime by going to **Settings | General** and accessing the activity titled **Welcome Robot Inventor**:

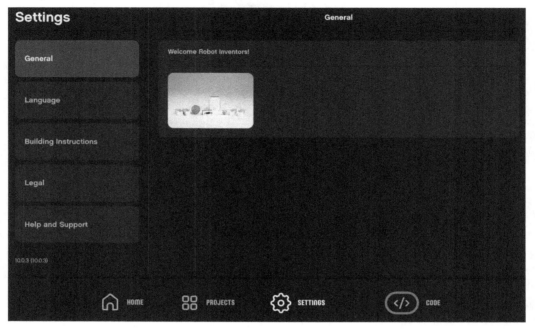

Figure 2.16 – The Welcome Robot Inventor activity found in Settings

Beyond this quick intro screen, you are prompted right away with the screen featuring the five robot builds, where you can choose any of them and build, code, and expand based on all the activities each robot provides.

This is a great time to explore these builds if you want to learn more about what this kit can do. These builds will give you ideas on how to build certain parts of robots as well as seeing how the coding platform operates. While this chapter has been mostly informative, take the time to build these models to experience what this robot kit is capable of making:

Figure 2.17 – The main screen with the five robot builds

Once you have had your fill of those robots, then it is time to begin to build your own projects. When you are ready to create your own builds and programs, you can scroll down to **Other** and get started on your ideas.

You will have the choice to program with blocks or Python, as shown in the following screenshot:

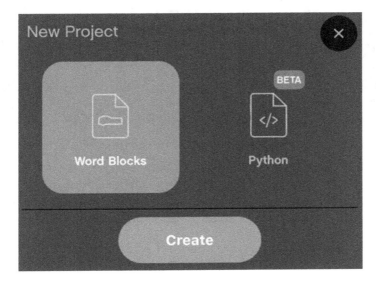

Figure 2.18 – You can choose blocks or Python

When you choose **Word Blocks**, you will get a Scratch-like interface to explore and build. This is a drag-and-drop application. You can see how the software looks when you choose the block coding option:

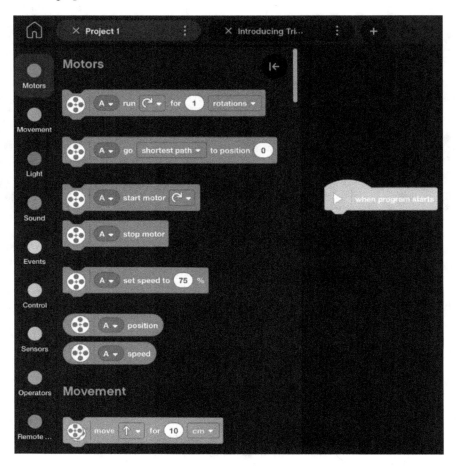

Figure 2.19 – The coding platform looks like Scratch when you choose blocks

The software is a Scratch-based programming platform. It uses a drag-and-drop coding process that many will already be familiar with if you have used Scratch, Blockly, MakeCode, or Code.org, and so you will be quite comfortable with the interface. The layout of colors on the black backdrop makes it easy to organize, find blocks, and explore the interface.

If you are looking to see even more blocks and add your Xbox or PlayStation controller, be sure to add the necessary extensions to your software by clicking on the gray-outlined blocks at the bottom of your screen, as shown here:

Figure 2.20 – Note the extensions at the bottom left of your screen to find these blocks

There is also a Python coding option within the software that will allow those who know how to program in Python to really push the boundaries of coding. This is a very important feature to bring this kit to the next level of experience and expertise. The following screenshot showcases what the Python coding interface looks like in the software if you wish to go down this route:

```
1  from mindstorms import MSHub, Motor, MotorPair, ColorSensor, DistanceSensor, App
2  from mindstorms.control import wait_for_seconds, wait_until, Timer
3  from mindstorms.operator import greater_than, greater_than_or_equal_to, less_than, less_than_or_equal_to, equal_to, not_equal_to
4  import math
5
6
7  # Create your objects here.
8  hub = MSHub()
9
10
11 # Write your program here.
12 hub.speaker.beep()
```

Figure 2.21 – Python coding interface within the software

I know that not everyone knows how to code in Python, so for the sake of this book, we will stick with the graphical interface for ease of understanding.

Having both options to code and program within the software is a huge bonus to prior kits. The option for text programming is going to allow the LEGO community to see some incredible projects being developed.

If you are new to Python, there is a manual icon on the side of the screen to help you see how the blocks look in Python, named Knowledge Base:

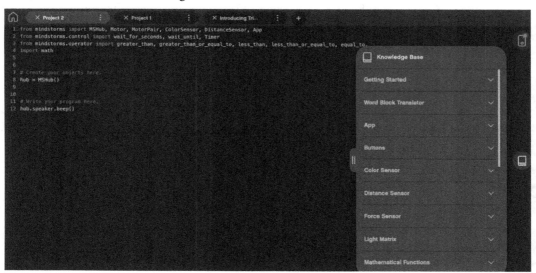

Figure 2.22 – Find the Knowledge Base icon on the right side of the screen

Once you click on the Knowledge Base icon, you will be provided with a menu of options to help with your learning and coding journey. Simply choose the topic you need help with, as shown in the following screenshot:

Figure 2.23 – Expanded help options within the notebook

The one fundamental difference to this programming environment compared to the LEGO SPIKE Prime kit is that lessons are missing. Of course, this is designed for retail instead of education like the SPIKE Prime, so that makes sense, but it's still worth pointing out. However, please check out the lessons to expand your skills as there is compatibility between the two. You can find the lessons here: `https://education.lego.com/en-us/lessons?products=SPIKE%E2%84%A2+Prime+Set`.

When you boot up the software, there are no introductions or any quick demos. Instead, you have to decide to build one of the five robots to get started, or hopefully, you have enough confidence to get started without guidance. One bonus of this software is that with each robot build, there are several activities to expand on the robots to learn some new build techniques and use to inspire the building of your own creations.

One crucial part of the programming software is being able to access data from your motors and sensors. You can access the Intelligent Hub through the software to gather all the data on your motors and sensors to be able to enhance your coding and build ideas.

On your software interface, at the top left of your screen, you can see some basic data or you can click on the Intelligent Hub icon to open up a new screen to dive deeper:

Figure 2.24 – Click the Intelligent Hub icon noted in this screenshot to access the data on your Intelligent Hub

There is a ton of potential in this kit as you continue to explore and unravel all that can be accomplished.

Creating a rock, paper, scissors wrist game

So far, you have been doing a lot of reading, so let's take some time to do a quick build that covers some of the concepts shared about this new and exciting kit. You are going to build a fun little game of rock, paper, scissors that you can wear on your wrist.

You will need the following parts:

- One Intelligent Hub
- 12 black connector pins
- One black *7x11* open frame
- Two black *5x7* open frames
- Two teal *9L* beams
- Two gray *H* connector brackets
- Eight gray connector pins with a stop bush

To start this build, find your Intelligent Hub:

Figure 2.25 – Intelligent Hub

Locate four black connector pins. Flip the Intelligent Hub over to the back side and insert the four pins into the middle pin holes on the top and bottom of the Hub:

Figure 2.26 – Black pin connectors on the Intelligent Hub

Locate your two black *5x7* open frame parts and attach the *5L* side to the pins you just inserted into the Intelligent Hub:

Figure 2.27 – Open frames added to the Intelligent Hub

It is time to locate the following parts:

- Two teal *9L* beams
- Four black connector pins

Using two black connector pins with each *9L* beam, secure the open frame and the Intelligent Hub with these beams:

Figure 2.28 – Black pins and 9L teal beams

Be sure to leave the bottom pin hole of the open frame open:

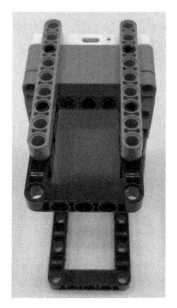

Figure 2.29 – 9L beams added to sides

Repeat this process by doing the exact same thing and adding the it to the other side of the Intelligent Hub:

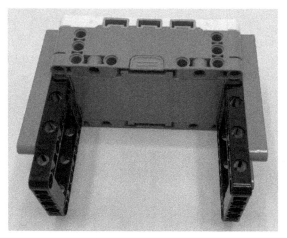

Figure 2.30 – Side view of the build so far

Locate the following parts:

- One black *7x11* open frame
- Four black connector pins:

Figure 2.31 – Open frame and black pins

Add two black connector pins to the middle pin holes on both sides of the *7L* side of the open frame:

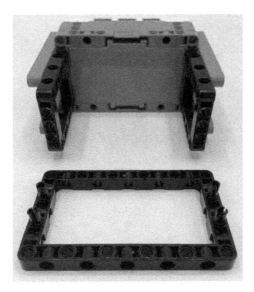

Figure 2.32 – Black pin added to the open frame

Connect this open frame to the bottom of the other open frames already connected to the Intelligent Hub:

Figure 2.33 – Open frame added to the bottom

You need to locate the following parts:

- Two gray *H* connector brackets

- Eight gray connector pins with a stop bush:

Figure 2.34 – Gray pins and H beams

Insert four of the gray pins to the bottom two holes on each side of the *H* bracket. Do this to both of the parts:

Figure 2.35 – Gray pins added to H beams

Use these parts to secure the bottom open frame to the sides of this build. If you want to add this to your wrist, insert your wrist first and then secure it with these parts. If you have a tiny wrist, then hold onto the side so it does not fall off when you shake it playing the game!

Figure 2.36 – Completed build

This is a very simple build, but it is designed to be quick and easy to assemble to be able to play your first game of rock, paper, scissors. It is now time to write some code and play the game!

Coding a rock, paper, scissors wrist game

You are now going to code this wrist game to be able to randomly choose rock, paper, or scissors. You can play it against yourself or use it against another human. If you have a friend that has a kit, then you can both build one and compete this way:

1. Using the default yellow **when program starts** block, add a purple **Light** block named **write Hello**. You will need to change the word from **Hello** to **Left**:

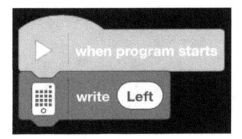

Figure 2.37 – "Left" being programmed to screen

2. Add two yellow **Events** blocks named **when Left Button pressed**. Make one that activates when the setting is set for the left button and the second block set for the right button.

3. Go to the pink **My Block** sections of the coding blocks and make two new blocks. Name one `start game` and the other `playagain`. Add these new blocks to the yellow blocks. Add the **start game** block for the left button and **playagain** for the right button:

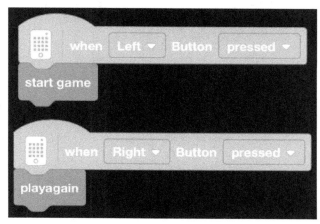

Figure 2.38 – Decision making with MyBlocks

4. In the previous step when you created these blocks, you should have seen two new pink blocks show up in your coding canvas named **define playagain** and **define Start Game**. Locate **define playagain**:

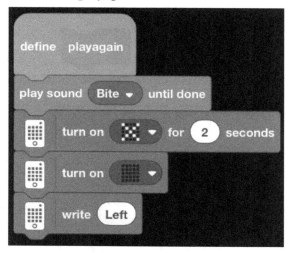

Figure 2.39 – playagain My Block

5. Under the **define playagain** block, add a sound effect by adding a purple **play sound** block named **play sound Cat Meow until done**. Change the audio file to one of your choice. Under this block, add a **Light** block named **turn on Smiley Face for 2 seconds**. Click the face and change the graphic to your choice. In this example, an X was made. Add another light block underneath this one, turning off all the lights. Finally, add a final purple **Light** block named **write Hello** and change **Hello** to **Left**.

6. You will follow a similar process for the other **define Start Game** block. Locate this pink block. Add a purple **play sound** block named **play sound Cat Meow until done**. Change the audio file to your choice. Add a purple **Light** block named **turn on Smiley Face for 2 seconds**. Change this block to the number 3 in the graphical interface and change it from 2 seconds to 1 second. Right-click the purple **play sound** block you just added and choose **duplicate**. Duplicate these two blocks two times so you don't have to keep dragging blocks. Change the 3 to a 2 and the other to a 1 to create a countdown timer. Last, create another pink **My Block** and name it Rps. Add this block to the end of this code:

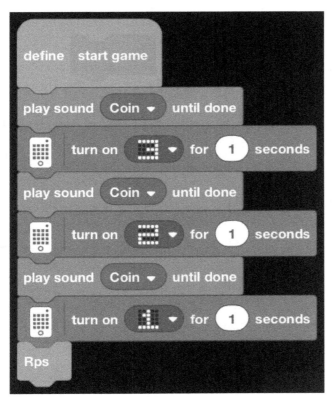

Figure 2.40 – start game My Block

The final step is to program the Rps block:

1. Add a purple **Light** block named **turn on** and change the smiley face to the four squares in the corners.

2. Add an orange **Control** block named **wait until**. Add a blue **Sensor** block of **Hub is shaken** to the diamond space.

3. Go to the orange **Variable** block and make a variable named Rps_Random. Add the **set Rps_Random** block to the code. Use a green **Operator** block named **Pick Random** and select numbers **1-3**.

4. Add an orange **Control** block named **If**. Drag in a green **Operator** block that compares with the = sign. On one side of the equals sign, add your **Rps_Random** block, and on the other side, insert the number 1.

5. Within that **If** block, add a purple **Light** block named **turn on** and turn on all the lights to symbolize paper.

6. Add one more purple **Light** block named **set Center Button light to** and choose a color.

7. Right-click this **If** block you just created and duplicate it two more times. For these two copies, change the numbers to 2 and 1. Change the design from paper (all lights) to a smaller square for rock for one, and for the other, design a pair of scissors.

8. Add an orange **Control** block named **Wait** and choose 5 seconds so that you have time to see your game choice.

9. Add a purple **Light** block named **write Hello** and change it to Right:

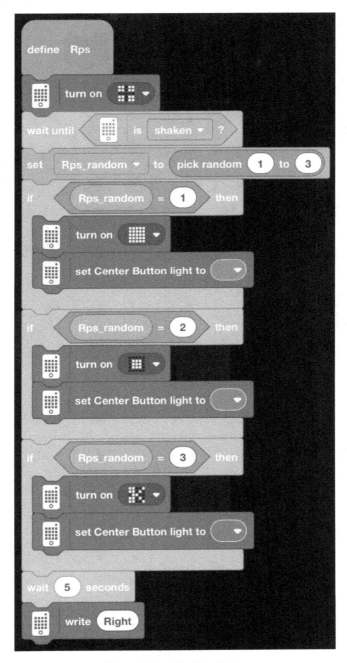

Figure 2.41 – Rps My Block

In the end, your code should look like this:

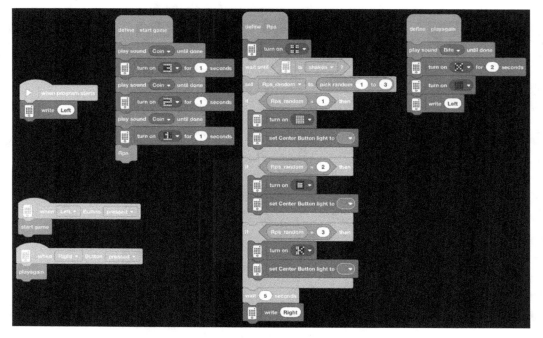

Figure 2.42 – Complete view of the code

How it works is the game will tell you **Left** on the screen to indicate to press the left button. This will trigger the **start game** My Block, which will do a countdown timer to show your choice. Once it counts down, it will then move to **Rps**, where the code will wait for you to shake the Intelligent Hub before displaying a choice of rock, paper, or scissors. After it displays the choice for 5 seconds, it will then tell you **Right**, so when you press the right button, it will reset the screen and wait for you to press left again to play the game.

Making your own game

Consider how you can take this simple and classic game and make it your own. Here are some suggestions that will allow you to use your imagination and build up some skills as well:

- Design your own icons for rock, paper, and scissors.
- Convert this to a flip a coin (heads or tails) game.

- Convert this game from rock, paper, scissors to the rolling of a die. Can you rewrite the code so that when you shake the Intelligent Hub it mimics the random roll of a die?

- Add an option where you can choose from the three games to play/use.

Summary

To wrap up this chapter, let's do a quick review of what we covered. We explored the overall look of the new LEGO Mindstorms Robot Inventor kit. We examined the parts and elements that come with the kit, along with the sensors. Additionally, we took some time to look at the programming software.

Now that we have a basic understanding of the kit and some featured elements, let's finally get to the building of robots. Let's take what we have learned to start building some fun smart robots to challenge our thinking and creativity.

If you have not taken the time to build any of the five robots that are in the software, I would encourage you to take some time to build them and explore the ideas shared. None of these builds are required for the builds in this book, but they do provide a good foundation for the parts and building.

A few of these builds will reference certain build features from these five builds to showcase how these ideas inspire new ideas.

In the next chapter, we will start with a robot arm and claw, a classic build that is always great to build to explore the parts, programming, and use of sensors.

3
Building an Industrial Robot Claw

Industrial robots have been around for a long time. In many cases, industrial robots are not the humanoid-looking robots we imagine when thinking of robots. Instead, many are robot claws that can do a wide variety of tasks: surgery, welding, assembly, painting, and more. In this chapter, you are going to build a robotic claw pick up a red ball that comes with the kit, to better understand how these claws work and operate. In the following screenshot, you can see what you will be building:

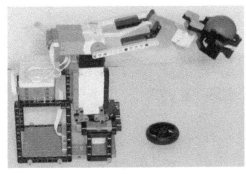

Figure 3.1 – Robotic claw

In this chapter, we will break down the build and program, as follows:

- Build the frame for the Intelligent Hub
- Setting up the motor frame to move right and left
- Setting up the motor frame to move up and down
- Framing the motor that operates the claw
- Writing the code

Technical requirements

For the building of the robot, all you will need is the Robot Inventor Kit. For programming, you will need the LEGO MINDSTORMS app/software.

Access to the code can be found here: `https://github.com/PacktPublishing/ Smart-Robotics-with-LEGO-MINDSTORMS-Robot-Inventor/blob/main/ Chapter%203%20Claw%20Code.lms`.

If you would like a more detailed photo-by-photo build process of the robot, please head here: `https://bit.ly/2NkkypN`

Building the claw

Before we build the claw, let's explore the strategy being used for these claws. There are many LEGO robotic claws to be found online. This one tries to do some things differently, as follows:

- The claw needs to be able to be controlled by a human.
- The claw needs to be able to move from side to side.
- The claw needs to be able to move up and down.
- The claw needs to be able to open and close the claw to grab various objects.

We are going to start this build using a large teal *11x19* base plate as the main building foundation for this robotic claw. Ensuring that we have a solid foundation is key, and the teal *11x19* base plate shown in the following screenshot is perfect for building on top of when designing an claw:

Figure 3.2 – The LEGO teal base plate

Let's build the robotic claw now, starting with the frame for the Intelligent Hub!

Building the frame for the Intelligent Hub

One part of this kit that is different from previous **Mindstorms** kits is that the wires for all sensors and motors are set to a specific length. In previous kits, we could attach various cable sizes as we built our bigger structures.

Because all wires are a set length that we cannot adjust, we must consider this creative constraint in the build design. With that being said, we need to build a frame to place the Intelligent Hub at a certain height to allow the motors to be able to reach the Intelligent Hub while in motion.

You will need the following pieces:

- Two black *11x15* open frames
- One black *7x11* open frame
- Four gray connector pins with bush stops
- Four black connector pins

The required pieces are shown in the following image:

Figure 3.3 – Overview of parts needed to begin the build

Start by adding the two black *11x15* open frames to the side of the teal base plate. Use the gray connector pins to hold them in place by inserting them through the pinholes into the sides of the teal base plate.

Using two black connector pins on each side, secure the black *7x11* plate to the top of the black *11x15* open frames, as illustrated in the following image:

Figure 3.4 – Building a stand for the Intelligent Hub using the open frames

Using two large open frames and one medium-sized open frame, we will assemble a standing desk for the Intelligent Hub. We will attach the Intelligent Hub to the top, where it will sit one row off the back of the base plate. The final step of this part of the build is to add the Intelligent Hub to the top of the frame.

Setting up the motor frame to move right and left

This section sets the foundation to the entire robotic claw. You will start by building a strong base for the claw to establish the motor that will allow the claw to move right and left.

You will need the following pieces:

- Intelligent Hub
- One motor
- Six black connector pins
- Two gray perpendicular connector pins, bent

Start by adding four black connector pins to the four corners of the bottom side of the Intelligent Hub, as illustrated in the following image:

Figure 3.5 – Pin placement on the underside of the Intelligent Hub

Go ahead and connect the Intelligent Hub to the top of the base you just assembled. It should lock into the *7x11* open frame, as illustrated in the following image:

Figure 3.6 – Stand for the Intelligent Hub

Using one motor, two gray perpendicular connectors, and two pins, we can secure the motor to the base, as illustrated in the following image:

Figure 3.7 – Parts needed to secure motor to base

Make sure your motor is properly secured to the base. To do this, add the gray connector pins to the sides of the motor, along with the black connector pins in the middle pinhole of the motor on both ends, as illustrated in the following image:

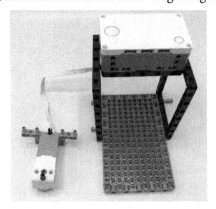

Figure 3.8 – Gray connector pins attached to the motor

When you connect the motor, we will place it three rows back from the front of the base plate. Place the black pins on the underside of the motor to really secure it to the base, as illustrated in the following image:

Figure 3.9 – Placement of the motor

Next, it is time to build a solid frame for the motor and turntable, for the claw to properly move. You will craft a table using the following pieces:

- One turntable
- Four blue connector pins
- One teal *3x3* Technic piece

The required pieces are shown in the following image:

Figure 3.10 – View of the unassembled turntable

To begin this part of the build process, start by sliding the *3x3* teal Technic piece in the middle of the turntable, on the gray side. Ensure the pinholes align with the gray pinholes of the turntable. Secure the teal *3x3* piece to the turntable using two blue connector pins on either side, as illustrated in the following image:

Figure 3.11 – View of turntable piece assembled

Locate the following parts to go along with this turntable piece:

- Two black *11L* beams
- Two gray connector perpendicular pins
- Two teal *3x3* Technic pieces

- One teal *3L* beam
- Four blue connector pins

The next screenshot provides a basic layout on how to attach all these pieces together, with a step-by-step description to follow:

Figure 3.12 – General layout of parts

The following steps align with the preceding image, starting from the top and working down:

1. Start with one black *11L* beam.
2. Add the two gray perpendicular pins to the outside edges.
3. Next, attach a *3x3* teal Technic piece to each of the gray pins.
4. Follow this up by adding two blue connector pins to the outside holes of the teal *3L* beams and connect these to the *3x3* teal pieces.
5. Before you finish this build, insert the turntable piece right into the middle of this part, as shown in *Figure 3.13*, using the blue connector pins exposed on the turntable.
6. Finally, secure it all together with the second black *11L* beam.

   The resulting build can be seen in the following image:

Figure 3.13 – Turntable fits in middle

This is what it should look like on the underside, to ensure you have things properly placed. The turntable should spin freely:

Figure 3.14 – Black connector pins in the second pinhole from the edges

If all is good, then find four black connector pins and add them to the black beams in the pinholes one hole from the end

Now that this piece is assembled, we will attach this to another open frame.

You will need the following pieces:

- Two teal *2x4 L* beams
- Two black *2x4 L* beams
- One *7x11* black open frame
- Four black connector pins

Add two black connector pins on both *11L* sides of the open frame, as illustrated in the following image:

Figure 3.15 – Black pins added to the open frame

Next, you will stack the turntable piece on top of this open frame, as illustrated in the following image:

Figure 3.16 – Stacking the turntable piece on the open frame

After these two build pieces are stacked, then go ahead and use the *2x4 L* beams and connect the turntable piece to the open frame, as illustrated in the following image:

Figure 3.17 – View of the built turntable piece

Go ahead and find the following pieces:

- One yellow *5L* axle
- One white connector piece
- Two black *5x7* open frames
- Four black connector pins
- Four gray connector pins with bush stops

The required pieces are shown in the following image:

Figure 3.18 – Yellow axle to begin to connect parts

Insert the white connector piece to the end of one side of the yellow axle. Insert the yellow axle through the middle of the turntable, securing it to the middle pinhole of the motor that is placed on the main teal base plate, as illustrated in the following image:

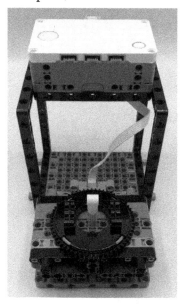

Figure 3.19 – The turntable will sit low

The following image shows the elements you should now have left:

Figure 3.20 – Parts needed for this build section

Using your *5x7* open frames, gray connector pins, and black connector pins, you are going to add these parts to the sides of the turntable piece to secure and mount it to the main base plate, as illustrated in the following image:

Figure 3.21 – Gray connector pins hold frames to base

The next step is to lock the motor to the turntable to allow the entire claw to move right and left. These parts will connect the top of the claw to the turntable.

You will need the following pieces:

- Four teal *T* Technic pieces
- Four blue connector pins
- Four black connector pins
- Two black *7L* beams
- One black *12L* axle
- Two gray axle bushes

To build these parts you will connect the *T* pieces to each of the black *7L* beams, using two blue connector pins. Both parts will be built with the *T* piece being on the outside of the black beam. You will build two of these parts with the *T* teal piece on the outside, as illustrated in the following image:

Figure 3.22 – T teal piece on the outside of the beams

You will then add each of these parts to either side of the turntable, locking them into place. This is illustrated in the following image:

Figure 3.23 – Side view of build model

Find the *12L* axle and two gray bushings. These are illustrated in the following image:

Figure 3.24 – Parts to secure all elements together

Slide the *12L* axle through the middle pinhole of the *T* pieces and through the white pin connector in the middle of the turntable. Secure the axle using the two gray bush stops on the ends of the axle, as illustrated in the following image:

Figure 3.25 – Holding together with gray bush stops

The final step in this build part is to now attach the final two teal *T* Technic pieces to the end of the black beams that are now on the turntable. Use two black connector pins on each one to attach, as illustrated in the following image:

Figure 3.26 – View of build at this current step

Your next step in this build is to build up the frame for the other motors, for the claw to be built upon.

To get started, you will need the following pieces:

- Four white panels
- Four blue axle pins
- Twelve black connector pins
- Four teal *3x5 L* beams
- Four black *3x5* beams

To begin, locate two white panels, and on each of them add two black connector pins, as illustrated in the following image:

Figure 3.27 – White panels for the claw

Using the black connector pins, attach the white panels to the teal *T* parts that are currently on the turntable, as illustrated in the following image:

Figure 3.28 – Two white panels added to the turntable

This is how the build will look from the side now:

Figure 3.29 – Side view of the build

With the build facing you, where the turntable is to the front and the Intelligent Hub is to the back, add a black connector pin and a blue axle connector pin to both white panels, as illustrated in the following image:

Figure 3.30 – Placement of connector pins

The last step to complete on this part of the build is to add two more panels, to complete the main structure of the claw. Note the parts to secure the two panels, using the *L*-shaped Technic pieces in the following image. One white panel will use the four teal *3x5 L* beams, and the other will use the four black *3x5 L* beams.

This is how it would look from the front after adding the panels:

Figure 3.31 – Third white panel added

This is how it would look from the other side of the panel:

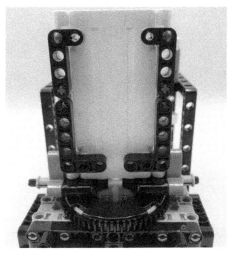

Figure 3.32 – Fourth white panel added

Here is how the build should look at this point in time:

Figure 3.33 – Top view of the white panels

Let's finish up this part with the final pieces. You will need the following pieces:

- Twelve black connector pins
- Three black *5x7* open frames
- Two blue connector pins

Begin by adding four black connector pins to the corners of the white panels on the top of the build, as illustrated in the following image:

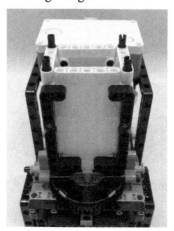

Figure 3.34 – Adding black connector pins to the panels

Using the two blue connector pins, insert them in two corners of one of the open frames, as illustrated in the following image:

Figure 3.35 – Parts for the base of the claw motor

Stack the three open frames together, using six of the black connector pins. Placement is not essential, but you just want to make sure they are securely held together. The last two black connector pins will be added to the top, between the two blue connector pins, as illustrated in the following image:

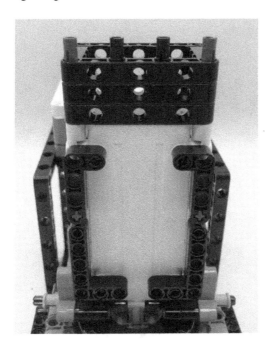

Figure 3.36 – Open frame stand for claw

Now that we have set up the motor frame to move left and right, let's see how to set it up to move up and down.

Setting up the motor frame to move up and down

You are now ready to add the two motors that will control the claw's upward and downward movements.

You will need the following parts:

- Two motors
- One gray *3L* axle
- Two teal *5L* beams
- Six black connector pins
- One teal *3x3* Technic piece

Grab two motors and connect them with a *3L* axle, as illustrated in the following image:

Figure 3.37 – Connected motors using 3L axle

Add them on top of the four connector pins, on top of the three open frames, as illustrated in the following image:

Figure 3.38 – Placement of motors on top of open frames

Using the two teal *5L* beams and four of the black connector pins, secure the motors together, as illustrated in the following image:

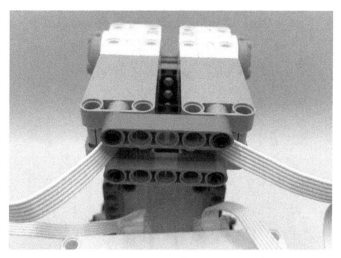

Figure 3.39 – Securing the motors together

At this point, you need to fold up and hide the wires. We will close off the wire and secure these *1x5* beams using one *3x3* teal Technic piece and two black connector pins, as illustrated in the following image:

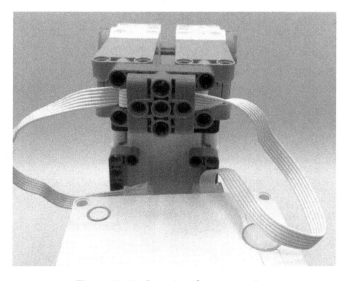

Figure 3.40 – Securing the motor wires

You can now plug these motors into ports *B* and *F*. If you have not already done so, you can also add the motor at the bottom of the base to port *C*. After you have connected the motors, let's keep building from the motors. Next, you will need to add a gray *3L* axle to the middle of each of these motors. After that, add a gray perpendicular connector pin to each motor. The result is shown in the following image:

Figure 3.41 – Robot claw main frame

This would be a great time before you continue building to run a test code, to ensure your claw can move from right to left and to tweak any adjustments that need to be made. Write a simple program moving the motor just to make sure it moves.

Framing the motor that operates the claw

You are now down to your final motor that will control the claw being able to open and close.

For this section of the build, you will need the following parts:

- One motor
- One gray *3L* axle
- Two black connector pins
- One teal *5L* beam

Start this build part by adding two black connector pins and the gray *3L* axle to the pin holes on the motor, as illustrated in the following image:

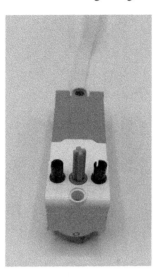

Figure 3.42 – Preparation for claw motor

Attach the teal *5L* beam to the connector pins that you just added to the motor in the previous step, as illustrated in the following image:

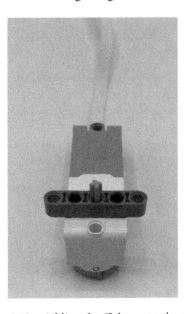

Figure 3.43 – Adding the 5L beam to the motor

You are going to continue to build out the claw on this motor. To do so, you will need the following parts:

- Two black connector pins
- Two black 45-degree beams
- One gray *3L* axle
- One black axle and pin connector

Start by adding the two black connector pins to the ends of the *5L* beam, as illustrated in the following image:

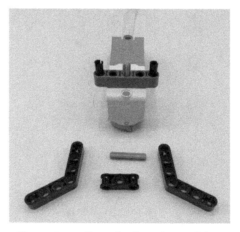

Figure 3.44 – Parts for first phase of claw

Using the first pinhole of the black 45-degree beams, add one pin to each end. On the 45-degree beam that is on your right side, insert the *3L* axle in the second pinhole and secure it using the black pin and axle connector piece, as illustrated in the following image:

Figure 3.45 – Base of the claw

Now, locate the following parts:

- One black *2L* pin axle connector
- Two tan axle pin connectors
- One gray *3x5* perpendicular *H*-Shape beam

You will connect the axle and pin connector to the motor using a *1x2* beam, as illustrated in the following mage:

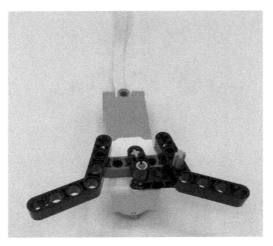

Figure 3.46 – Top view of the base of the claw

Take the second tan axle pin connector and add it to the other 45-degree beam using the axle hole, as illustrated in the following image:

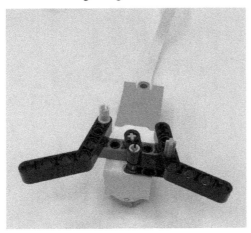

Figure 3.47 – Connector placement for movement

Additionally, you will hold everything in place while allowing movement of the claws by layering on the *H*-Shape Technic element. Again, check the placement of the connector pins to allow the claw to move properly. The result should look like this:

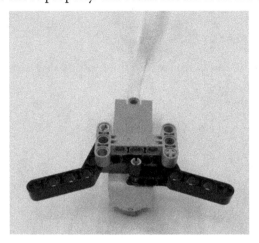

Figure 3.48 – H shaped piece to help with claw movement

Let's get this claw all put together. You will need these pieces next:

- Four black 45-degree beams
- Two blue pin axle connectors
- Two brown *3L* axles with end stops

The required pieces are shown in the following image:

Figure 3.49 – Parts for second phase of claw build

Insert a brown *3L* axle through the end of each of the 45-degree beams in the axle hole. Be sure the 45-degree beams are bent to face inward as these are part of your claw mechanism.

Insert a blue axle pin connector into the end of the 45-degree beams that are already attached to the motors.

Connect the 45-degree beams that have the brown *3L* axle to the 45-degree beams that are attached to the motors. You will start to see the formation of a claw. The next image provides a visual of what your build will look like after this series of steps:

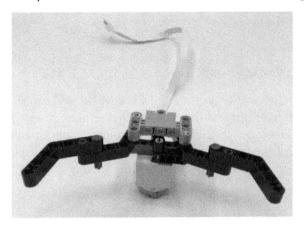

Figure 3.50 – Connecting 45-degree beams together

Find two more 45-degree black beams and attach them to the underside, where the brown *3L* axle is still showing. Connect by using the axle hole of the 45-degree beams, as illustrated in the following image:

Figure 3.51 – Second-phase build of claw view

Let's keep building this claw to ensure it can grip the red ball that comes with the kit. You will need the following pieces:

- Two black 45-degree beams
- One black connector pin
- One blue axle pin connector
- One black *3L* beam
- One dark-gray axle pin connector
- One blue connector pin
- Two yellow *5L* axles
- Four black rubber *1x2* axle connectors

To start this part of the claw, begin by attaching a 45-degree beam to the right side of the claw. Use the black connector pin and the blue axle pin connector to secure it into place. Note how the beam will stick out from the inside. The black connector pin is inserted in the pinhole to the right of the brown axle. The blue connector pin is used to the right of the black connector pin, as illustrated in the following image:

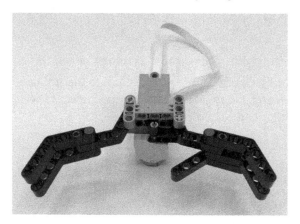

Figure 3.52 – Adding support bracket for an object on the right claw

Let's move to the left side of the claw. For this side, you will need the following parts:

- One 45-degree black beam
- One *3L* black beam
- One dark-gray pin axle connector
- One blue connector pin

The required parts are shown in the following image:

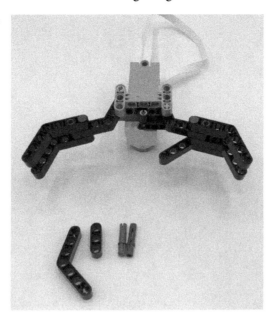

Figure 3.53 – Parts for support bracket for object on left claw

Start by attaching the *3L* beam to the 45-degree beam. Use the dark-gray connector pin on the end of the 45-degree beam using the axle hole. Add the *1L* side of the blue connector pin to the pinhole next to the axle hole, as illustrated in the following image:

Figure 3.54 – Assembled parts for support bracket for an object on left claw

This part will connect to the underside of the left side of the claw, as illustrated in the following image:

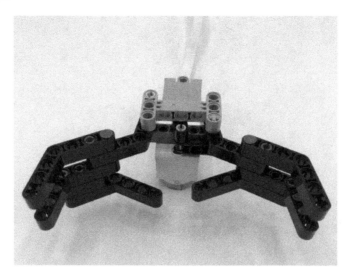

Figure 3.55 – Assembled view of support brackets on the left claw

Secure all the parts of the claw together using the yellow *5L* axle pieces. Insert each axle onto the end of the claw, as illustrated in the following image:

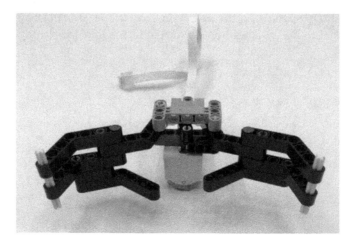

Figure 3.56 – Yellow axles added to the claw

The last part to this claw is to attach the two black rubber axle parts to the ends. These parts help with gripping the red ball upon pickup and are shown in the following image:

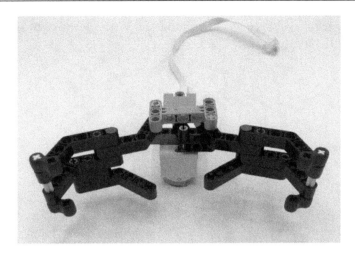

Figure 3.57 – Grippers to hold the ball

When the robot claw rises to its full extent and brings the ball straight up, the claw cannot contain the red ball without the rubber attachments. Using the rubber elements and an extra holding mechanism that does not get in the way of the claw moving, we can finish up the claw to better stabilize the red ball while in motion. Note that you can adjust and modify the claw to your own needs if you want to grab other items besides the red ball.

Keep in mind that you can create the claw to your liking at this point in time. This claw was designed to pick up and move the red ball in the kit. You might need to adjust the claw if you wanted to grab different items or objects.

The final step of the claw is to attach this claw mechanism to the rest of the robot body. You will need the following parts:

- Two white *13L* beams
- Two teal *5L* beams
- Two black *5L* beams
- Two black *3L* beams
- Two black *9L* bent beams
- Six blue connector pins
- Four black connector pins
- Two dark-gray pin axle connectors

In the following image, you will see what the build looks like on the right side, with the elements needed on the left side:

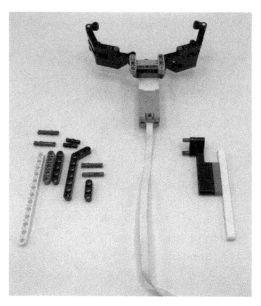

Figure 3.58 – Claw support beams to add to the main frame

You will build two of these parts so that you have one for each side of the claw motor, to be attached to the main base of the robot.

Start with the white *13L* beam. Insert two blue connector pins in pinholes *3* and *7*, as illustrated in the following image:

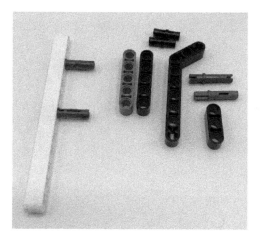

Figure 3.59 – Blue pin connectors added to white beam for brackets

Attach the teal and black *5L* beams to the blue connector pins. Add two black connector pins to the black beam, as illustrated in the following image:

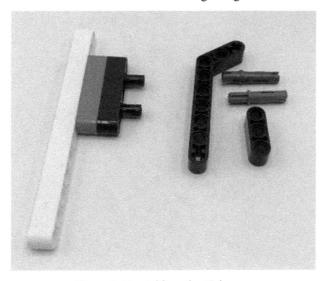

Figure 3.60 – Adding the 5L beams

Next, add the bent *9L* beam, with the bent piece facing up. Add the dark-gray connector pin into the axle hole of the bent beam and the blue connector pin to the base of the bent part of the beam. Finally, slide the black *3L* beam over these pins, as illustrated in the following image:

Figure 3.61 – Assembled view of the bracket

Repeat this process for the second piece, and just be sure that both pieces have the white beam on the outside of the build, as illustrated in the following image:

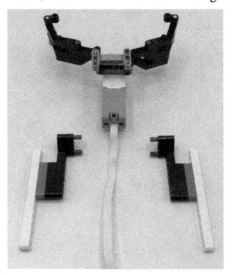

Figure 3.62 – Layout of the brackets for the claw

Once you have checked to make sure they are built properly, then go ahead and connect to the claw on the back of the motor. Just to double-check, you should have the following two parts built at this point in time, as seen in the next image:

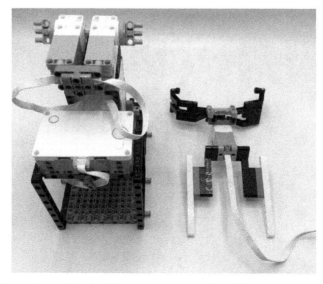

Figure 3.63 – Two build components you should have at this point

The final step of this build is to add the claw attachment to the main frame. Connect the claw to the motors at the top of the robot claw on the base. You can adjust the claw on the *1x13* Technic beam, but I have found this setup to be most effective when the motor is not slipping and is moving properly. The result is shown in the following image:

Figure 3.64 – The claw attachment set on the robot

A key detail here is the wire of the claw motor. It needs to be run between the two *B* and *F* motors to reach the Intelligent Hub properly, to allow for proper movement. You will connect the claw motor to port *D*. Check your wires by moving the claw to the right and left, checking for snags with the wire.

Here is what the robotic claw should look like from the left when completely assembled:

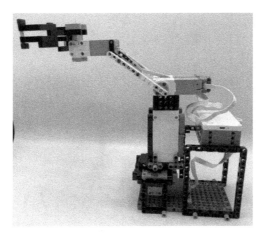

Figure 3.65 – Left-side view of the completed robotic claw

This is how it should look from the front:

Figure 3.66 – Front view of the completed robotic claw

This is how it should look from behind:

Figure 3.67 – Rear view of the completed robotic claw

And this is how it should look from the right:

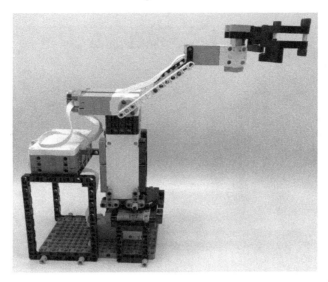

Figure 3.68 – Right-side view of the completed robotic claw

Now that your claw is complete, it is time to move into the coding to bring the robot claw into use.

Writing the code

For this build, we are going to focus on the remote app coding only. This will be a program that will allow you to control the robot using the remote-control feature of the app to move the claw right, left, up, and down, and to open and close the claw.

Overall, this program is fairly simple to develop and is created to be easily adaptable for you to remix to meet your needs. Use this sample code to make sure everything works, and then begin to tweak the code to make it work to your needs. Make sure you have the proper ports plugged in, and then move into the code.

Identifying the ports

If you have not plugged in your motors yet, then let's get them plugged in to the proper ports. You will plug the motor that moves the claw to the right and left to motor port C. The motor that controls the opening and closing of the claw will plug into port D. The two motors that control the arm of the claw to go up and down will use ports B and F. Once you have the motors plugged in, then double-check that the motors are plugged in correctly.

You can check that your motors are properly plugged in by checking the **Port View** in the software, as seen in the following screenshot:

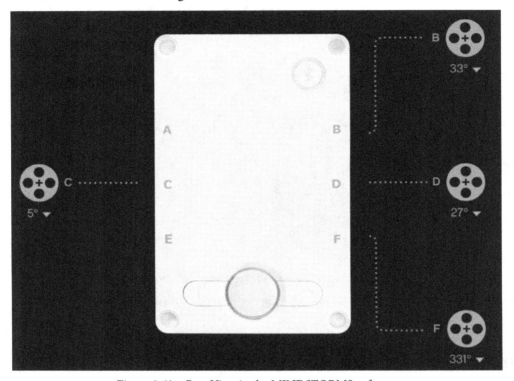

Figure 3.69 – Port View in the MINDSTORMS software

It is time to write the program so that you can control the claw.

Remote-control robot program

To get started with this program, let's go ahead with the following steps to make the robot come to life:

1. Open up the **MINDSTORMS** software.

2. Click on **Projects** at the bottom of the menu bar.

3. Scroll down to **Other**, click or press the icon, and then select **Create New Project**.

4. On the **New Project** window, select the **Word Blocks** option, and click on **Create**.

5. Before we can activate the **Remote Controller** blocks, we have to turn on the commands we need. In order to do this, we must click on the joystick icon on the right-hand side of the screen, as illustrated in the following screenshot:

Figure 3.70 – Joystick icon on the right-hand side of the screen will pull up the control panel

6. This will give you the screen needed to build your remote control. Once you are here you need to select the edit icon, which is the pencil in the upper right-hand corner, as shown in the following screenshot:

Figure 3.71 – Choose the pencil icon to create your controller

7. On this **Remote Control** window, select the teal **plus** icon at the bottom of the screen to add the necessary widgets. In this project, we will select two of them. We will add the **D-Pad** and the **Horizontal Slider** widgets. Feel free to use a different widget configuration to control your robot, but for the sake of this example, we will use these two widgets. The different widgets available are shown in the following screenshot:

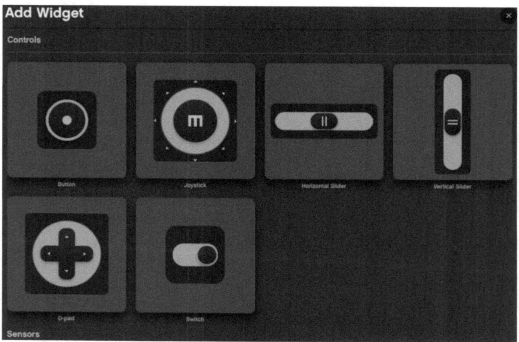

Figure 3.72 – Choose the Joystick and Button widgets

This is what you will need for your controller layout:

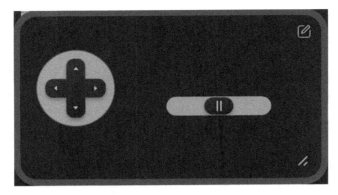

Figure 3.73 – Controller layout

Be sure to select the teal check to save your design, as shown in the bottom-right corner of the following screenshot:

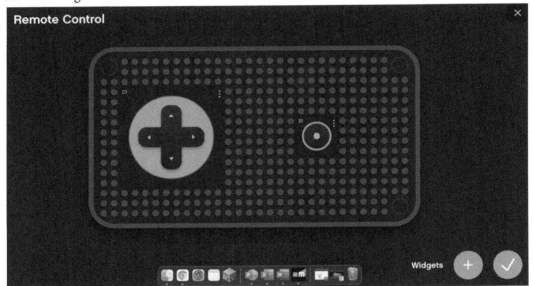

Figure 3.74 – Teal check in bottom-right corner to save settings

You can also move widgets around the grid to place them where you would like for your remote controller. Each person has preferences, so adjust to your needs. *Figure 3.73* shows the controller layout I prefer to give an example of what the controls can look like on the remote control.

8. Let's start with what will happen when the program starts. As mentioned earlier, the code is simple and is open for you to make it unique. Essentially, what we want to do here is make sure that the robot is aligned and ready for use. Using the blue **motor block** section add two blocks, adjusting the speed of motors C and D to a low speed to align to position 0. This will move the robot to a starting position of facing forward, ready to get to work. The speed is low so that it does not go crazy, and this keeps the movement smooth. The startup code is illustrated in the following screenshot:

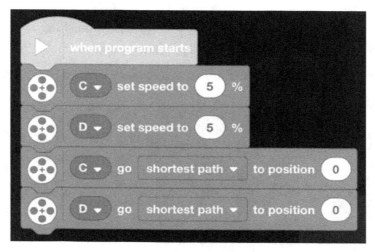

Figure 3.75 – The basic startup code

9. The next step is to get the robot to move up, down, right, and left. I have organized the coding blocks to mimic the directional pad. Again, the speed of the motors is low, at around **5%**, to keep movement slow and steady. The code is pretty straightforward, using the blue motor blocks and pink movement blocks. Please note, as seen in the following screenshot, that you are using some pink movement blocks that are part of the **extension** section of the code. Please activate the **More Motor** and **More Movement** blocks to find the blocks used in this program:

Figure 3.76 – Extensions block menu

Test your code and make sure the claw moves to your liking. You might need to tweak the numbers a bit to make it work the way you want. I prefer a code layout that mimics the controls, as you can see in the following screenshot:

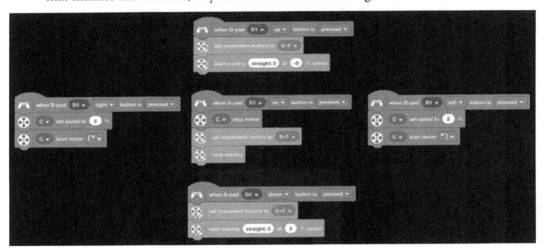

Figure 3.77 – The code

10. The final step is programming the claw to open and close. Using the teal remote-control blocks to activate the horizontal slider, we will add some simple code to have the motor open and close to our liking.

The speed is low, and we can duplicate the code and change the direction of the motor when the slider is high compared to low. The code blocks in the following screenshot showcase the low speed **of 5%** to move the claw:

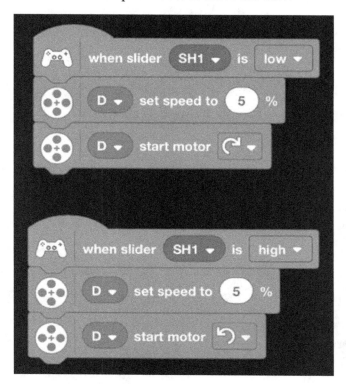

Figure 3.78 – Claw code

In the end, your code will look something like this:

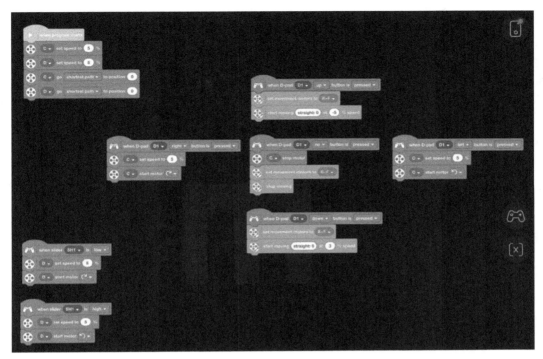

Figure 3.79 – Final display of code

And that is it! You did it. You built a nice-looking and working robot claw. Now comes the fun part, which is to remix the claw to make it your own. Let's look at some ideas.

Making it your own

This is the part I love, and I hope you do too. This robot is just the beginning of the fun. It is now time for you to take this framework of the robot build and sample code, to make it unique to your talents and imagination.

Here are a couple of ideas to consider applying to this robot:

- Add sensors to trigger autonomous robot decisions. For example, could you add a color sensor so that as the claw moves, it is waiting to detect red to stop and pick up the ball and move to another location?

- Add lights of the **light-emitting diode** (**LED**) matrix on the Intelligent Hub to provide insights or cool new looks as the robot operates.

- Add sound effects to make it sound like an industrial robot.

Summary

In summary, we explored the concept of industrial robots by building a robotic claw that can pick up a red ball and transport it to another location. Industry continues to rely on robotics to achieve production goals. Additionally, we explored how to have several motors working together to create an actual working claw. This is a classic build that must be done with any new robotic kit!

Let's now head to the next chapter and explore a whole different world of robotics by building a guitar!

4
Building a LEGO Guitar

Entertainment is an important aspect of our lives and well-being. Music is a great hobby and interest for people and it also creates career-making opportunities. As technology continues to advance in our lives, we see it increasingly being used to create music, music experiences, concerts, and more.

This chapter will be combining robotics and music by using the Robot Inventor kit to make a guitar that is playable and codable to our unique needs.

With a gaming industry that was impacted by the awesomeness of **Guitar Hero** and the likes of many other music games, let's create our own instrument that will allow you to jam out to your favorite song.

Here is what your guitar will look like by the end of this chapter:

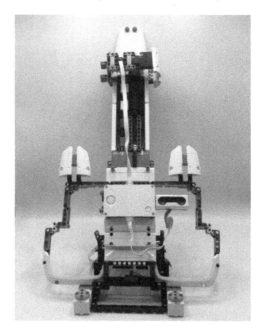

Figure 4.1 – The final guitar build

In this chapter, we will break down the guitar build and coding into the following sections:

- Building the stand (to place the guitar on when not in use)
- Building the guitar
- Writing the code
- Playing the guitar
- Making it your own

Technical requirements

For the building of the robot, all you will need is the **Robot Inventor kit**. For programming, you will need the LEGO MINDSTORMS app/software.

Access to the code for this chapter can be found here:

```
https://github.com/PacktPublishing/Smart-Robotics-with-LEGO-
MINDSTORMS-Robot-Inventor/blob/main/Chapter%204%20Guitar%20
Code.lms
```

If you would like a more detailed photo-by-photo build process of the robot, please head here to view the images: `https://bit.ly/3czErS3`.

Building the stand

Before we build the actual guitar, we will start with building a stand to place the guitar when it is not in use. The stand is not a super-detailed creation as it uses the elements left over from the guitar build, but it serves a purpose and achieves the necessary function.

The base will look like this when complete:

Figure 4.2 – The stand for the guitar

Let's start building it!

Building the base

To get started, you will need the following pieces:

- Two black *11x15* open frames
- Two black *3x5* L beams
- Four black connector pins

The required pieces can be seen in the following image:

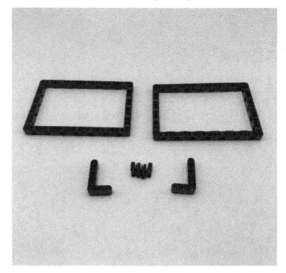

Figure 4.3 – Pieces needed for the stand

You will start by grabbing two of the open frames and securing them together using the *3x5* L beams. This part is the main frame of the stand. You will stand them in a perpendicular fashion. Use two black connector pins with each of the L beams, using one pin on the 3L side of the beam and another on the 5L side of the beam, as illustrated in the following image:

Figure 4.4 – The open frames connected

Next, locate the following pieces:

- One teal *T* beam
- Three black connector pins

The teal *T* Technic piece is going to help secure the open frame together. Place the black connector pins on the ends of the *T* piece and in the middle pin hole of the middle beam of the *T* piece. Secure this piece to connect the two open frames together, as illustrated in the following image:

Figure 4.5 – T beam for support

Let's keep building the frame up with the following pieces:

- Two gray *8L* axles with stops
- One white axle connector
- Two black connector pins
- Two blue pin axle connectors
- Two black *9L* bent beams
- Two black *11.5* double-bent beams

Next, you will build two arms that will allow you clip the guitar stand to better hold it in place and keep it from slipping down the stand. The clip sits on the main body of the guitar, as you can see in *Figure 4.1*.

You will connect the double-bent beams and single-bent beams together using one black connector pin and one blue pin axle connector. Note the build on the right side of the following image to see how it should look:

Figure 4.6 – Clip build for guitar stand

Repeat the same steps for the other clip. You should now have these two clips assembled, as illustrated in the following image:

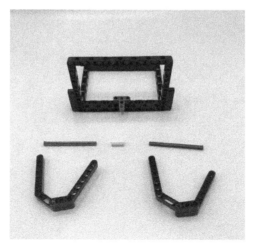

Figure 4.7 – Clips to help hold the guitar in the stand

Use the *8L* gray axles and the white axle connector to attach these clips to the base that we just built using the open frames. Insert a gray *8L* axle through the pin hole on each side of the open frame. Before you connect them with the white-axle-connector piece, be sure you slide a clip onto each gray axle. Once you have done that, then connect the two axles using the white-axle-connector piece. You should then have this piece connected through the open frame, as seen in the following image:

Figure 4.8 – Axles connected together

The guitar has some weight to it, and therefore we need a counterweight for the stand so that it does not tip over. The kit does not come with weights by nature, but we can rethink the use of the motors to serve as weights. Even better is that the motors can clip quite easily to the side of the stand. We will use two motors, but if you need to add more, it is quite easy to add motors to the front of the stand as extra weight.

You will need the following pieces:

- Eight black connector pins
- Two teal *2x4* L beams
- One white *13L* beam
- Two motors
- Two gray perpendicular connectors

To begin with the counterweight build, add two black connector pins to the upper corners of the back of the stand, as illustrated in the following image:

Figure 4.9 – Black connector pins in top corners of open frame

Add a teal *2x4 L* beam to the ends of the white *13L* beam using a black connector pin for each *L* beam, as illustrated in the following image:

Figure 4.10 – 2x4 L beams connected to the white beam

Using the black connector pins you recently added to the back of the frame, attach this piece to the stand, as illustrated in the following mage:

Figure 4.11 – Beams attached to the open frame

Locate your motors and add two black connector pins to each motor, as illustrated in the following mage:

Figure 4.12 – Prepping the motors

Secure the motors to the side of the stand using these connector pins. Once you do that, add the two gray perpendicular connectors to secure the wires so that they are out of the way, as illustrated in the following image:

Figure 4.13 – Wire organization

Now that you have added some counterweight, you need to add some additional support to the back of the stand to provide additional structural support in order to keep the stand from toppling over when you place the guitar onto the stand.

You will need the following pieces:

- Four black *11L* beams
- Twelve black connector pins
- One white panel
- One white curved panel

The required pieces can be seen in the following image:

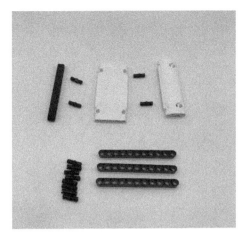

Figure 4.14 – Parts for the next aspect of the build

The next part of this stand's construction is to make sure that it does not fall backward. The motors are important, but they can't prevent the guitar from falling over completely. You will need to add some support to the back of the stand to help keep the guitar propped up.

Start with one of the black *11L* beams. Secure the white panel to this beam. Next, add the white curved panel. Lastly, add the three black *11L* beams. Using two more black connector pins you will be able to attach this to the back of the stand, as illustrated in the following image:

Figure 4.15 – Building the back support for stand

Here is how it should look assembled to the back of the stand:

Figure 4.16 – The back support for the guitar stand

You can now build the next part of the stand, and that is the part that gives the guitar something to lean on while it is in place. Using some of the basic elements and avoiding the pieces we need for the guitar build, we can create a nice piece that looks somewhat like a guitar neck to match the stand with the guitar itself.

You will need the following pieces:

- Sixteen black connector pins
- Two blue connector pins
- One white panel
- Two angled white panels
- Two small-angled white panels
- One black *11L* beam
- One teal *9L* beam
- Two teal *3x3* Technic pieces

Start by adding two black connector pins to the top of the open frame on your stand, as illustrated in the following image:

Figure 4.17 – Front view of stand with pins added to the top

Next, assemble the white panel and angled white panel pieces together using black connector pins. Use two connector pins for each panel and two for the bottom of the white panel. Add a teal *9L* beam across the bottom to hold all the pieces together, as illustrated in the following image:

Figure 4.18 – Angled white panel build for the stand

Add a black and blue connector pin to each of the angled white panels and then attach a *3x3* teal Technic piece to each of these pins. The black connector pin goes to the outside bottom pin hole and the blue connector pin goes to the inside pin hole on the bottom, as illustrated in the following image:

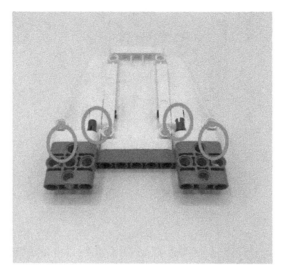

Figure 4.19 – 3x3 beams added to the build

Secure these *3x3* teal Technic pieces using black connector pins and one black *11L* beam across the bottom, as illustrated in the following image:

Figure 4.20 – Black beam for further support and height

Locate your two small-angled white panels and four black connector pins. These can be seen in the following image:

Figure 4.21 – Using the small-angled white panels

Connect these small-angled white panels to the *3x3* teal Technic pieces, as shown in the following image. Add a black connector pin to the bottom of each of these small-angled white panel pieces:

Figure 4.22 – Adhering angled white pin to the teal 3x3 pieces

Let's wrap up this build portion by finding the following pieces:

- Eight black connector pins
- Three teal *9L* beams
- One black *11L* beam
- One black *7L* beam

The required pieces can be seen in the following image:

Figure 4.23 – Additional pieces needed

The previous image provides a layout of how all these parts fit together. Basically, we are trying to add some height to this portion of the stand to properly support the neck of the guitar. Add these pieces together by starting one of the teal *9L* beams. Using two black connector pins, attach a second teal *9L* beam to this beam. Repeat the process by adding another two black connector pins to the teal *9L* beam to be able to attach the *11L* black beam, as illustrated in the following image:

Figure 4.24 – Parts added together

Add these beams to the black connector pins on the small-angled white panels. After you do that, then go ahead and hold it all together by adding another teal *9L* beam across the back using the two blue connector pins that are already on the build, as illustrated in the following image:

Figure 4.25 – Securing the build with teal beams

Add two more connector pins to the white panel at the top and attach the black *7L* beam, as illustrated in the following image:

Figure 4.26 – Final addition of the black beam to the build

You should now have two parts assembled, as follows:

Figure 4.27 – The two parts you should have built at this point in time

Go ahead and attach the part with all the white panels to the stand using the black connector pins that are sitting on top of the open frame, as illustrated in the following image:

Figure 4.28 – Two parts of stand put together

You have to add one last detail to the stand. Find the following pieces:

- One blue connector pin
- Two blue axle pins
- Two medium-angled white panels
- One teal *5L* beam

The required pieces can be seen in the following image:

Figure 4.29 – Layout of the top piece of the stand

Assemble the parts as shown in the preceding image, using the blue connector pin to join the teal *5L* beam in the middle of the angled white panels. Once you have the blue connector pin holding the two white curved panels together with the teal *5L* beam in between them, then go ahead and add the two blue axle pins to the bottom of each white curved panel so that you can add this piece to the top of the stand. This piece will attach to the top of the guitar stand.

Here is the completed build of the stand:

Figure 4.30 – Top piece added to stand

Here is a front view of the stand at this point in the build:

Figure 4.31 – Front view of stand

Go ahead and set this stand aside as we build the guitar that will eventually use this stand. But so that you can get a sense of how this works, check out how the guitar sits in the stand by referring to the first image in this chapter labeled *Figure 4.1*.

Building the guitar

You will build the guitar in sections. Each section will provide a basic framework for the guitar, but please keep in mind that with all the builds you have the space and opportunities to build it the way you want. In terms of the guitar, the key pieces to customize it will be the body of the guitar, the top of the neck of the guitar, and the **light-emitting diode** (**LED**) lights. Additionally, when you get to the coding, you can really fine-tune it to have the guitar sound just the way you want it to.

Let's get started with the building.

Assembling the neck

We will start with the neck of the guitar. For this, we are going to use the *1x3* colored Technic pieces to create sections for the color sensor to detect. The color sections are reminiscent of the Guitar Hero guitars, but instead of pressing buttons we will use the color sensor to detect the colors.

You will build five different colored sections for the fretboard. This maximizes the length of the color sensor wire and gives the player five different notes to play. Let's build one together.

You will need the following pieces to build one of these guitar panels. You will build five of these in total, so repeat this part element five times to complete the guitar neck:

- One black *5x7* open frame
- Three black connector pins
- One teal *3x3* Technic piece
- Two colored *3L* beams of the same color (use red for this first build)
- Four blue connector pins

The required pieces can be seen in the following image:

Figure 4.32 – Parts needed to build a color panel for the fretboard

Start this part of the build by adding two black connector pins to the side of the *3x3* teal Technic piece. Connect a *3L* beam to the connector pins. Next, add a black connector pin in the middle pin hole of the *3L* beam. Attach the second *3L* beam.

The result can be seen in the following image:

Figure 4.33 – 3x3 piece attached to two 3L beams

That piece will fit inside the *5x7* open frame. Secure it in place using the four blue connector pins by using the *2L* side of the pin to connect the frame to this piece, as illustrated in the following image:

Figure 4.34 – One fretboard color panel complete

You will repeat this same process, assembling five of these open frames. In the book example, you will use the colors red, green, white, blue, and yellow. Go ahead and repeat this process until you have five completed panels.

The following image shows five parts being assembled:

Figure 4.35 – You will need five of these parts built using different colors

Once you have the five parts assembled, then it is time to connect them all together to begin building the fretboard of the guitar. Line them all up with the blue connector pins sticking out on the sides, as illustrated in the following image:

Figure 4.36 – The color sections of the fretboard

Once you have all five colored sections completed, you will connect them all using the following pieces:

- Four white *13L* beams
- Four black *7L* beams
- Fourteen black connector pins
- One gray connector pin
- Two black *7x11* open frames

Start by adding two white *13L* beams on either side of the open frames you just assembled, as illustrated in the following image:

Figure 4.37 – White beams added to hold the fretboard together

Next, find your two *7x11* open frames and add two black connector pins to the *7L* side of each of the open frames, as illustrated in the following image:

Figure 4.38 – Pins added to the open frames

Additionally, using six black connector pins, you will then connect all four black *7L* beams together, as illustrated in the following image:

Figure 4.39 – Pins added to open frames

Connect the two open frames together by adding the four black *7L* beams to the middle of them. Add the gray connector pin to the middle pin hole of one of the open frames, and the opposite open frame should have two black connector pins on the outside pin holes on top, as illustrated in the following image:

Figure 4.40 – Support frame built for the fretboard

Now, you can add the open frame build to the fretboard. Make sure when you connect the support frames to the back side that you make the open frame flush with the sections that have the color block, leaving the one extra space open. Note this in the following image, where the gray connector pin is open and shown:

Figure 4.41 – Open frames under the fretboard

When you have added the support frame, you can continue to build the guitar neck. You will need the following pieces:

- Four teal *9L* beams

- Eight blue connector pins

Combine the four teal *9L* beams together using the four blue connector pins, as illustrated in the following image:

Figure 4.42 – The teal pieces combined

This piece will connect to the top side of the fretboard covering the open frame below that has the gray connector pin showing, as illustrated in the following image:

Figure 4.43 – Teal pieces added to the bottom of the fretboard

The final step for the fretboard is to add the top part, where the strings can be tightened on a regular guitar. We don't have strings, but we can still add the top part to make sure it looks incredible. You should have the following pieces remaining to build this part of the guitar:

- Two black *5L* beams
- One white medium panel
- Two angled white panels
- Four blue connector pins
- Two black connector pins

The required parts can be seen in the following image:

Figure 4.44 – Parts for the top of the guitar neck

Connect the black *5L* beams to smooth out the fretboard and the top of the guitar. There is also another one on the back, securing the white pieces. Use the blue connector pins to join the black *5L* beams to the fretboard and the top of the guitar. Use the black connector pins to join the white panels, as illustrated in the following image:

Figure 4.45 – Completed fretboard

The final touch before you move on to the next build structure is to add eight gray connectors of ½ size. These will be added to the fretboard on the teal *3x3* Technic pieces. Please note how the layout of these pieces alters on each teal *3x3* piece.

> **Important note**
>
> Note the placement of the small gray connector pins. These are tough to get out, so be careful!

The result can be seen in the following screenshot:

Figure 4.46 – Addition of the gray pins for the slide bar

Once you do that, then add ten black connector pins to the fretboard. Two pins go to each *3x3* teal Technic piece, as illustrated in the following image:

Figure 4.47 – Connector pins added to each 3x3 teal piece

Now that you have the basic layout of your guitar fretboard complete, you need to add the guard rails that will be part of the color sensor slide component to play your guitar.

You will need the following pieces:

- Two teal *9L* beams

- Two black *15L* beams

- Two black smooth flat *8L* beams

- Two black smooth flat *6L* beams

The required pieces can be seen in the following image:

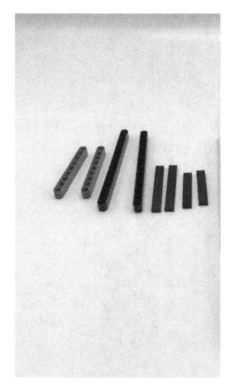

Figure 4.48 – Pieces needed for final section

To build the guardrails, use the *9L* teal beams and the black *15L* beams, and add them to the black connector pins. One teal and one black beam go on each side. Next, add the flat pieces between the rails. Note that these pieces will lay over the teal beams using the gray ½ connector pins connected to the fretboard.

The result can be seen in the following image:

Figure 4.49 – Fretboard with guardrails for the slide bar

Ensure everything is solid and connected. If you need to go back and support any elements further, you should do so now.

Let's move on to the color sensor build component so that we can actually play the guitar.

Building the color sensor slide bar

The next piece we need to build is the slide bar, which will allow the color sensor to slide up and down the fretboard to read the colors of the *1x3* Technic pieces we just put on the fretboard.

The device you are building will allow you to take it off when not in use and also provides a nice place for your thumb while playing.

To get started, you will need the following pieces:

- One color sensor
- Two gray *H*-shaped beams
- Five black connector pins

The required pieces can be seen in the following image:

Figure 4.50 – Pieces required for the color sensor slide bar

The *H* pieces are incredible for building out the structure of the frame. Add four black connector pins to the sides of the color sensors. Use these pins to attach the *H* beams to either side of the color sensor. Add one black connector pin to the right side of this piece, as illustrated in the following image:

Figure 4.51 – H pieces connected to sensor

Next up, you will need the following pieces:

- Two teal *5L* beams
- Four black connector pins
- Two blue pin axle connectors
- Two black round axle connectors
- One teal round spacer connector pin
- One gray *3L* axle

The required pieces can be seen in the following image:

Figure 4.52 – Parts to build out the slider

On one side, you will add the component that will slide up and down the smooth black flat pieces on the fretboard. Use two black round axle connectors by connecting them together, using a *3L* axle piece with one teal round spacer connector pin between them. Next, add the teal *5L* beams across, using the blue axle connector pins and black connector pins. This will give the proper distance for the sensor to read the colors of the fretboard.

The result can be seen in the following image:

Figure 4.53 – The sliding element that slides against the flat black pieces of the fretboard

Add this piece to the right-side *H* gray beam:

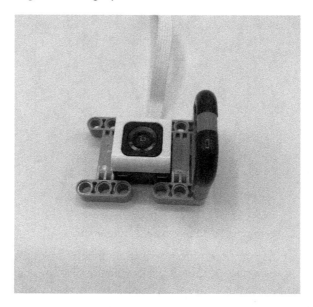

Figure 4.54 – The slider added to the color sensor

Next, locate the following pieces:

- One teal *5L* beam

- One teal *9L* beam

- Two blue connector pins

The required pieces can be seen in the following image:

Figure 4.55 – Parts to build out the opposite side of the piece

On the *H* beam on the left that currently does not have any pieces built upon it yet, you will start by adding one *5L* teal beam, followed up with one *9L* beam, using the blue connector pins. This is illustrated in the following image:

Figure 4.56 – Addition of the beams

Let's finish up the slide component by locating the following pieces:

- Four black connector pins
- Two gray perpendicular bent pins
- Two teal *T* beams
- Four teal round spacer connector pins

Add the four black connector pins to the top of the *9L* teal beam, as follows:

Figure 4.57 – Adding the black connector pins

Next, you will be building two of the same parts designed to hold the color sensor slider onto the fretboard. To do this, you will start with the gray perpendicular connector pins and add two teal round spacer connector pins to two of the pins and the *T* beam on the other two connector pins, as illustrated in the following image:

Figure 4.58 – Two parts to hold onto the fretboard

These two parts will need to be attached to the slide component to finish up this current build part, as illustrated in the following image:

Figure 4.59 – Slider attachments added to the color sensor

The slider will use the teal round connectors as rollers along the fretboard. Before we add this piece to the guitar, you still have more to build on the slide bar before completing this section of the guitar, but let's set this part aside while we build the next part of this slider, which will give your hands a place to rest.

You will start with the following pieces:

- Two white curved panels
- Two black *5L* beams
- Six black connector pins
- Two blue connector pins
- Two teal round axle connectors

The required pieces can be seen in the following image:

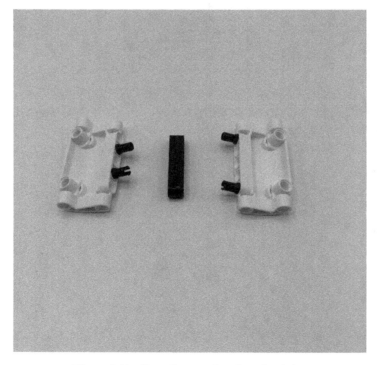

Figure 4.60 – Parts for your hand on the slider

Connect the two white curved panels together using the black *5L* beam and four black connector pins, as illustrated in the following image:

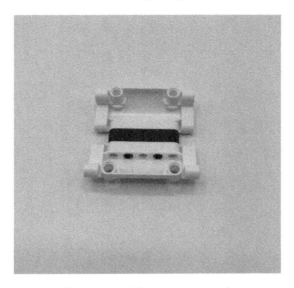

Figure 4.61 – The parts put together

Next, add two black connector pins to the underside of one of the white curved panels. On the other panel, add two blue connector pins. On the blue connector pins, add a black *5L* beam and then two teal round connectors, as illustrated in the following image:

Figure 4.62 – Round connectors added

Again, you are using the teal round connectors to slide along the fretboard, like you did in a previous step. Next, find the following pieces:

- Three black *5L* beams
- Two black *3L* beams
- Two blue connector pins
- Four black connector pins

The required pieces can be seen in the following image:

Figure 4.63 – Parts to finish up the rest of this build

The previous image not only gave you a visual of the pieces, but also how they go together. You will build these pieces to the white panel that has the black connector pins. Stack the *5L* beams followed by the two *3L* beams. Add a black *5L* beam to the black connector pins on the white panel piece. Use two more black connector pins to add another black *5L* beam. Do the same thing again, using two black connector pins to add the third black *5L* beam. Lastly, use the blue connector pins to secure the two black *3L* beams to these three black *5L* beams.

The result can be seen in the following image:

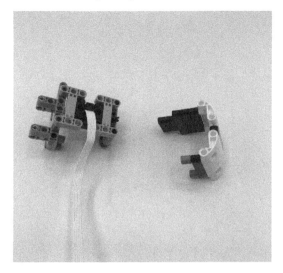

Figure 4.64 – The two parts for the slider

This new piece will connect the color sensor build you built previously. It slides and connects to the side where the black round connector part is on the color sensor. It will connect to the gray *H* beam.

This is how the completed build looks on the underside:

Figure 4.65 – Completed build of the slider underside

This is how it looks from the top:

Figure 4.66 – Completed build of the slider topside

At this point in the build process, you should now have these two pieces assembled, as follows:

Figure 4.67 – Fretboard and slider

The color sensor build will wrap around the fretboard. The white curved panels wrap around the edge of the fretboard. The black round connectors with the teal round connector in the middle will slide on the flat beams on the fretboard. Finally, the left side will connect along the white beam edge by ensuring the white beam sits between the teal round connectors on the gray perpendicular pins.

The result can be seen in the following image:

Figure 4.68 – Slider added to the fretboard

The last little final touch to this section is to use two blue axle pins to connect to the two teal round axle connectors. Add these to the top of the fretboard, as follows:

Figure 4.69 – Teal knobs added to give that guitar-string-nut look

Now that your fretboard is complete, let's get the rest of the guitar body completed so that you can rock out!

Assembling the guitar body

This is where you get to spice up the guitar to your liking. For the sake of this example you will build a basic outline of a guitar, but please know that from here, you can design a guitar to your own liking.

Let's get started!

You will need the following pieces:

- One Intelligent Hub
- One teal base plate
- Eight black connector pins
- Two gray connector pins with bush stops
- One white panel
- Two teal *2x4 L* beams
- Two blue pin axle connectors

You will begin with the teal base plate that comes with the kit. This is shown in the following image:

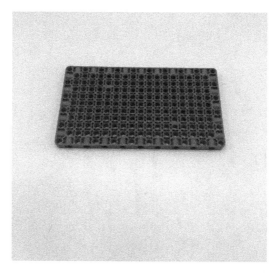

Figure 4.70 – Teal 11x17 base plate

Add two black connector pins to one side of the base plate and four black connector pins to the white panel, along with two gray connector pins to the top side of the white panel, as illustrated in the following images:

Figure 4.71 – White panel and teal base plate prep

Attach this white panel to the base plate. Add it to the same side you added the two black connector pins on the side. Be sure you leave two rows of space open from the edge, as shown in the following image. Connect the white panel to the base plate using the gray pins:

Figure 4.72 – Adding the white panel to the base plate

Next, slide the Intelligent Hub next to the white panel and connect it using the two black connector pins. Then, find the *2x4 L* beams, two black connector pins, and the two blue pin axle connectors. These can be seen in the following image:

Figure 4.73 – Parts needed to secure the Intelligent Hub to base plate

Secure the Intelligent Hub to the base plate using the *2x4 L* beams and connector pins, as follows:

Figure 4.74 – The start to the body of the guitar

You need to extend the size of the guitar body beyond the teal base plate. You will use some of the white panels to do this.

You will need the following pieces for this portion of the build:

- Ten black connector pins
- One white panel
- One white skinny panel
- One white curved panel
- One distance sensor

Begin by adding four connector pins to the base plate in the corners of pin rows on either side, like this:

Figure 4.75 – Pin placement on the teal base plate

Next, add four black connector pins to one of the white panels. Two will go on the top and two on the side, as illustrated in the following image:

Figure 4.76 – Prepping the white panel

Slide this white panel onto the edge of the base plate and then secure these two parts together with the white skinny panel, like this:

Figure 4.77 – Adding the flow pattern to the build

Use the two black connector pins that have not been used yet to add the white curved panel. The connector pins are used to join the Intelligent Hub to the white curved panel. The result can be seen in the following image:

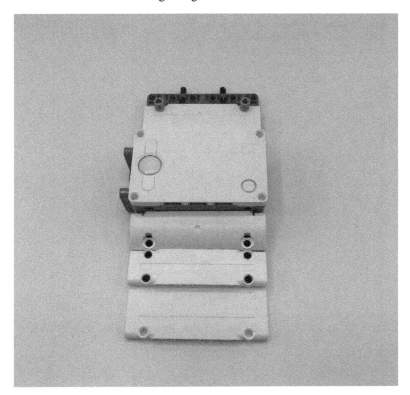

Figure 4.78 – Body build layout

Go ahead and attach the distance sensor to the side of the base plate and Intelligent Hub. This is an optional part of the guitar, depending on how you play your guitar. This is a good time to add it before you build out around the rest of the body. The distance sensor can be used for a variety of purposes, which we will explore in the coding section. Later, if you decide you don't need it then it is easy to remove it, but for now let's add it so that you have it to experiment with.

The result can be seen in the following image:

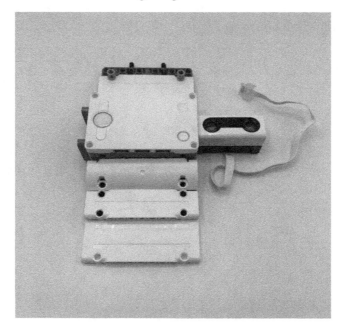

Figure 4.79 – Distance sensor added to the build

It's time to build the outer frame of the guitar body. You will need the following pieces to do this:

- Three teal *9L* beams
- Two black *7L* beams
- One black *15L* beam
- Two blue connector pins
- Sixteen black connector pins
- Two black double-bent beams
- Two black *3x5 L* beams
- Two teal *3x5 L* beams
- Four blue axle connector pins
- Two red connector pins with bush stops

Start with the *15L* beam. Attach one of the teal *9L* beams using the blue connector pins on both ends of the beam so that it is centered in the middle of the *15L* beam. Add the two remaining teal *9L* beams on either side, using the black connector pins to connect them to the black *7L* beams lined up on either side of the *15L* beam.

The result can be seen in the following image:

Figure 4.80 – Connected beams

Next, you will use the black double-bent beams and the black *3x5 L* beams added to this previous structure to build out the frame. You will need to use two black connector pins to connect the build you just assembled, as well as two black pins to connect the black *3x5 L* beams to the double-bent beam to hold it in place.

At this point, you will have the teal *3x5 L* beams and four black connector pins left, as can be seen in the following image:

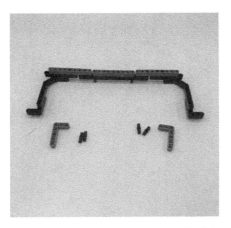

Figure 4.81 – Black L beams and double-bent black beams added

Here is how the frame looks when the teal *3x5* beams have been added to both sides using black connector pins:

Figure 4.82 – 3x5 teal L beams added

Continue to build out the body. Use the black double-bent beams and two blue axle connector pins. Also, add a red connector pin with bush stop with another blue axle pin connected to the top of the red pin to secure the piece in place, as illustrated in the following image:

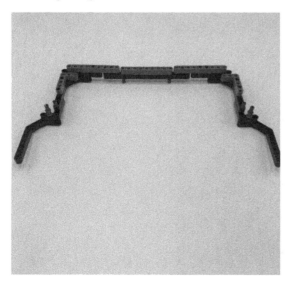 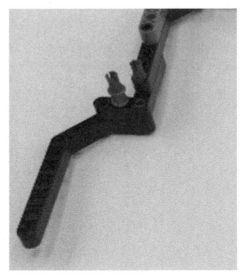

Figure 4.83 – Double-bent beams added

This is the part where you can begin to have fun with your guitar body if you want to design your own style. For now, let's start a new part list to finish up the rest of the guitar body build, as follows:

- Two teal round connectors
- Six black connector pins
- Two teal *2x4 L* beams
- Two teal *3x5 L* beams

Add a black connector pin to the corner slot of each of the *2x4 L* beams. Connect each of these to the corners using the blue connector pins that are available. The result should look like this:

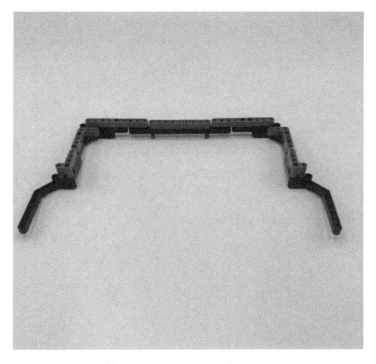

Figure 4.84 – Securing the parts

Using two black connector pins for each of the two teal *3x5 L* beams, add them to the black double-bent beams on the frame, as follows:

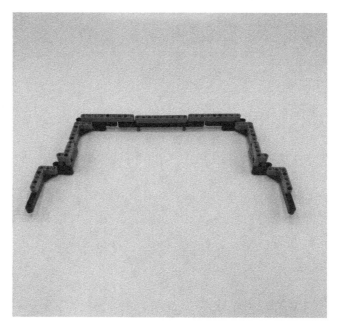

Figure 4.85 – 3x5 teal beams added to frame

You are getting close! Can you hear your favorite song start to play in your mind? Go ahead and find the following pieces to continue building out the guitar body:

- Two gray double pin and axle connectors
- Four white round connectors
- Two white bumper panels
- Two blue axle connector pins
- One black *15L* beam
- Two red connector pins with bush stops
- Two gray connector pins with bush stops

Add two white round connectors to one side of each of the gray double pin and axle connectors. Use this connector to connect the latest *3x5* teal beam to the rest of the frame. The result should look like this:

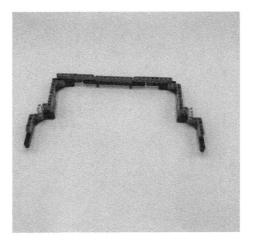

Figure 4.86 – Parts added to balance out layers of frame

Use the two blue axle connector pins to connect the white bumper panels to each side of the frame. Secure the two bumper frames using the *15L* black beam, and secure these pieces together using the two red connector pins. Finally, add two gray connector pins to each inner part of the white bumpers.

The result should look like this:

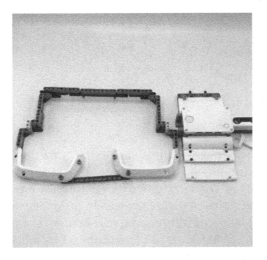

Figure 4.87 – Using bumper panels for the guitar frame!

Now, connect the guitar body frame to the Intelligent Hub build using the pins that are available and secure all the parts.

The result should look like this:

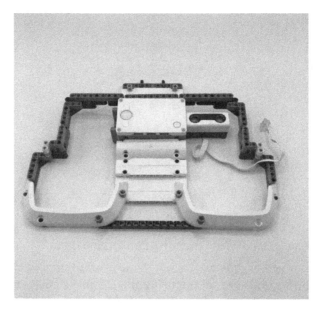

Figure 4.88 – Adding the Intelligent Hub to the guitar frame

Let's now add a little flair to the guitar body. We need to bring it to life just a bit more, so go ahead and find the following pieces:

- Eight blue pin axle connectors
- Four black round elbow connectors
- Four blue connector pins
- Two teal *3L* beams
- Four white medium-angled panels

You will build two pieces that will give some detail to the guitar body. The next image has one complete version and another one with the parts laid out to show how to assemble these. To build this out, start by connecting two blue connector pins through the pin holes of the teal *3L* beam. Use these pins to secure the teal *3L* beam between the two angled white panels. Next, add the blue axle pins to both axle holes of the black round elbow connectors. Attach two of these black round elbow connectors to the bottom of both angled white panel pieces. Have a look at the following image for an overview of this:

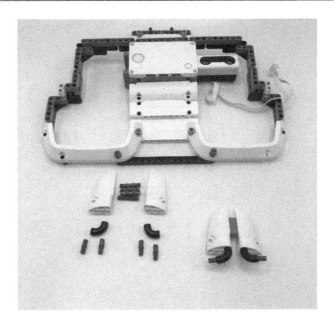

Figure 4.89 – Building out the corner pieces of the guitar frame

Add these parts to the top corners of the guitar body, as follows:

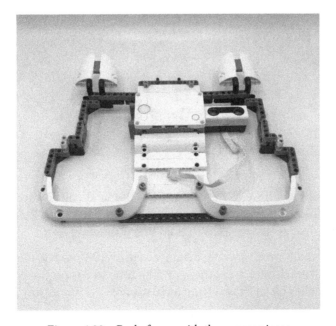

Figure 4.90 – Body frame with the corner pieces

You need a few more support beams to hold things together properly, so find the following pieces:

- Four blue axle connector pins
- One black *15L* beam
- One black *11L* beam

Add the blue axle connector pins to the tops of the gray and red bush connectors, and then attach the beams across the bumper panels.

The result should look like this:

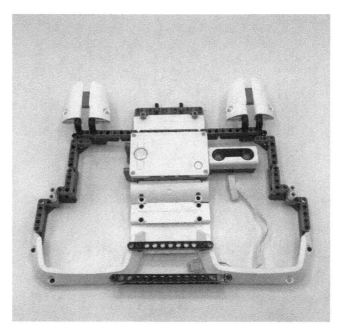

Figure 4.91 – Guitar body complete

Finally, it is the moment you have been waiting for—the final guitar step. Go ahead and add the fretboard to the body, and begin your rock-and-roll dreams! The fretboard slides into the body and connects with the pins to hold everything in place.

Plug the color sensor into port **C** and the distance sensor into port **D**. Go ahead and strengthen any parts you wish to strengthen, or take time to design the body the way you want your guitar to look. This is a great time to customize the guitar to your liking.

The final build of the guitar can be seen here:

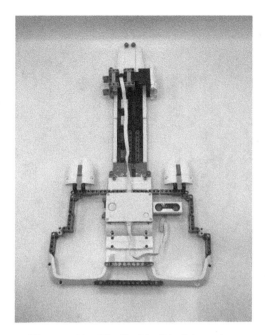

Figure 4.92 – The final build of the guitar

Now that our guitar is built, let's write the code for it!

Writing the code

The coding for the guitar is based on a very simple premise but allows for a complete individual interpretation on how you want to play the guitar and how you want the guitar to sound.

The program we are writing as an example will showcase some possibilities, but utimately, you should be brave and tinker around to get the guitar to sound how you want. The beauty of music is to express yourself the way you want to. This is your moment! Combining coding and music is an exciting combination of awesome.

The ports

There is not a lot to plug in for this build. You will connect the distance sensor into port **D**. You will also add the color sensor plugged into port **C**.

The following screenshot illustrates this:

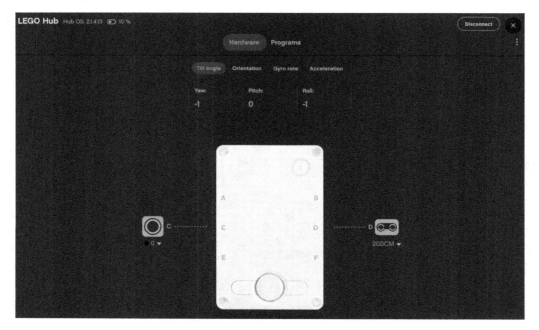

Figure 4.93 – Port view in the MINDSTORMS software

The basic layout of the program will follow this structure for each of the colored items on your guitar fretboard.

You will start by adding the yellow event block called **when**, shown in the following screenshot:

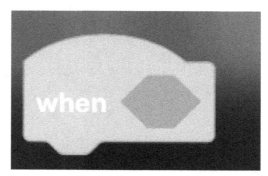

Figure 4.94 – Event "when" block

Inside the grayed-out area, you will add a logic **and** block, which is illustrated in the following screenshot:

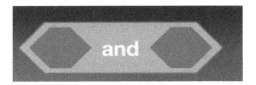

Figure 4.95 – Logic "and" block

Inside each of the empty spaces of this logic block you will add two conditions, using the **Sensor** blocks. First, you will add the **color** sensor block and will set the color to the first color on your fretboard. This is illustrated in the following screenshot:

Figure 4.96 – Sensor block for the color sensor

The second sensor condition will be the buttons on the Intelligent Hub itself. For my part, I found out I really preferred the right-button press, but you can adjust this to meet your needs. When you drag the button-press block over, it is in **Left button** mode by default, as illustrated in the following screenshot. You will need to click the arrow next to the word **Left** and select **Right** to change it:

Figure 4.97 – Sensor block for the button press on the Intelligent Hub will default to Left

Next, you need to add some extension blocks to be able to code music. Click on the extension block icon at the bottom left of the programming menu. From there, install the **Music** blocks, which can be seen in the following screenshot:

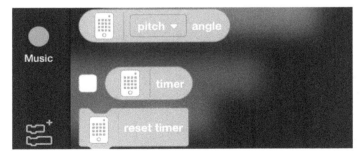

Figure 4.98 – Extension blocks located in the white-outlined blocks at the bottom left of the screen

The **Music** extension block provides you with a nice selection of ways to play music. You can experiment around to have the guitar play the notes and music that you prefer. You can have a lot of fun tinkering around, tuning your guitar to how you want it to play and sound. Some of the music options can be seen here:

Figure 4.99 – The Music extension block provides many options for playing music

In the next screenshot, you can see how the program comes together to play the notes for each color reading. I really liked the sound of the choir, for some reason. I found some basic sheet music for a song I knew I could handle (I am not musical at all) and changed all the notes to reflect what was needed to play the riff of *Smoke on the Water* by *Deep Purple*.

Additionally, I coded the LED lights on the Intelligent Hub to display the note or chord being played with each color, as illustrated here:

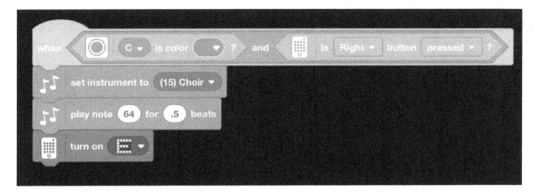

Figure 4.100 – The basic code of the guitar for each color

Once you have one color coded, you simply right-click on the selection of blocks and duplicate it four more times. For each one, you change the color of the color sensor and the note being played. This is illustrated in the following screenshot:

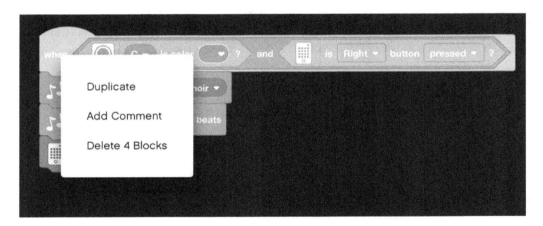

Figure 4.101 – Right-click so that you don't have to code each block over and over

Now that the code is ready, let's play it!

Playing the guitar

The beauty of Bluetooth is that you can continuously tinker with your code while you play your guitar and you do not need to be tethered to the computer. The music comes from the computer, so make sure your audio is turned up.

While playing the guitar, you can adjust how the music plays. I tried several options to find what I liked and share them with you here:

- Tweak your code so that the sensor plays the color it sees right away. The downside is that the guitar plays every note if you need to skip a color.

- Instead of using the right-button press to play a note, I used the distance sensor to activate the notes. I liked this at first, but I am too clumsy and kept triggering the sensor when I did not mean to. The distance sensor is shown here:

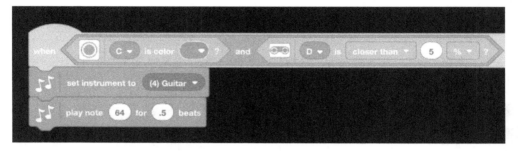

Figure 4.102 – Using the distance sensor to trigger sound

- I used the **tap** feature of the Intelligent Hub when it is tapped, the note would play. Again, I found a button press to be easier, but I did use this option for some time.

Now that the guitar is built, coded, and playable, it's time to customize it to your own needs!

Making it your own

I can't wait to see how you design your guitar and how you play it. Here are a few other ideas that you could use to make your own custom guitar:

- You could use the **play sound** block and import your sounds. Using the **Record sound** option, you could pull power chords from the internet and record them to yourIntelligent Hub. Using the **Edit sound** option allows you to further customize the sound.

- If you are talented, you could record yourself playing the actual chords/notes and pull that into the code.

The **Cat Meow 1** sound is shown in the following screenshot:

Figure 4.103 – Be creative and develop some unique sounds

- You could also experiment with using a block—such as the **change pitch** block—to change the pitch of a sound if the distance sensor is triggered or you tap the Intelligent Hub, or maybe add a motor and spin the motor.

Here's an example of the pitch effect being changed:

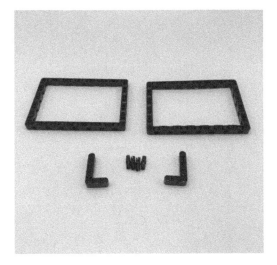

Figure 4.104 – Using distance sensors to tweak sounds such as a wah-wah pedal effect

The possibilities are endless! Have fun. Rock out. Enjoy your build!

Summary

In summary, we explored how to make an instrument with a robotics kit, and we remixed the idea of a robotics kit to make a musical instrument. There is great power in taking something we all know and love and trying to make a robotic version of it. We explored some new build techniques by using some of the basic elements that are found in the kit to create new ideas, such as the guitar slider.

Finally, we explored the coding by taking what is a simple coding program but understanding the many different ways we can take some simple code and make it work to our personal liking.

In the next chapter, you will explore another aspect of life to see how you can adapt ideas taken from nature to build a robot with a killer instinct, by making a scorpion.

5

Building a Scorpion

Biomimicry is the study and application of creating products, systems, mechanisms, and solutions to problems based on biological processes and functions found in nature. It is incredible what we can learn from plants and animals to find solutions to our own problems.

One of the many fascinating animals on our planet is the scorpion, a creature that has some features perfect for robot building. In this chapter, you are going to build a scorpion robot designed around the famous features of this creature. In particular, you will be building the stinger and a body style similar to that of a scorpion, along with some additional features that the kit provides.

Here's what your build will look like by the end of this chapter:

Figure 5.1 – Completed Build

In this chapter, we will break down the build and program into the following sections:

- Building the scorpion body
- Building the tail
- Adding the color sensor detection triggers
- Building the scorpion claws
- Building the scorpion exoskeleton
- Designing the tail
- Writing the code
- Making it your own

Technical requirements

For the building of the robot, all you will need is the **Robot Inventor kit**. For programming, you will need the LEGO MINDSTORMS app/software.

Access to the code for this chapter can be found here:

App code:

```
https://github.com/PacktPublishing/Smart-Robotics-with-LEGO-
MINDSTORMS-Robot-Inventor/blob/main/Chapter%205%20Scorpion%20
Controller%20Code.lms
```

Sensor code:

```
https://github.com/PacktPublishing/Smart-Robotics-with-LEGO-
MINDSTORMS-Robot-Inventor/blob/main/Chapter%205%20Scorpion%20
Sensor%20Code.lms
```

If you would like a more detailed photo-by-photo build process of the robot, please head here to view the images: `https://bit.ly/3rNjwkY`.

Building the scorpion body

The beauty of this robotics kit is that you can easily get started with any type of build because of the new pieces that are included. You are going to use the large LEGO *11x19* teal base plate as the main frame of the scorpion. This will be a vital piece where you will add motors to the wheels for movement, along with adding the entire top build of the scorpion. As with many builds in this book, you are utilizing this element to provide a base plate to hold everything together in a solid structure and format.

You can see what the base plate looks like in the following image:

Figure 5.2 – Starting with teal base plate

One of the LEGO pieces not found in this kit is a **LEGO Technic Steel Ball Caster** ball, or even the plastic version found in the **SPIKE Prime kit**. You will have to design a new way to operate your robot. What a wonderful design challenge! While there are plenty of wheels to use, a scorpion does not look like a scorpion if it is all decked out with wheels. You will use two wheels and then hide the other wheels underneath. This build will have you use a modified version of the two tiny wheels used in the software build model named **Tricky**. You need your robot to be able to pivot and rotate when sensing danger, so this is a nice adaptation since you don't have the caster ball that would make this very easy to do.

Establishing the the base

Let's start off by getting the wheels attached to the bottom of the base and adding the Intelligent Hub. You will need the following pieces:

- Two brown *5L* axles with stop
- One white axle connector
- Two white pin axle connectors
- Two tan axle pins
- Two black *2L* round connectors
- Two black smooth wheels
- Two black axle connector pin perpendicular double pieces

The required pieces can be seen in the following image:

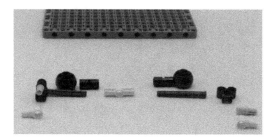

Figure 5.3 – Layout of how the parts go together for wheels

The preceding image shows a basic flow of how to connect all the pieces. To start, slide the black axle and connector pin perpendicular double piece onto each of the brown axles through one of the pin holes. Add a tan axle pin into the axle hole of this piece.

The result can be seen in the following image:

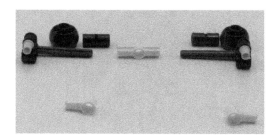

Figure 5.4 – Building two of the same builds and putting them together

After you add this part, then add the smooth wheel onto each axle, followed by the black round connector. You should now have enough of the brown axle left to connect the two sides together using the white axle connector, as illustrated in the following image:

Figure 5.5 – Wheels joined together

Finally, add the white connector pins to each of the tan pins for this part to be completed. You can see the result in the following image:

Figure 5.6 – White connector pins added to be able to join to base plate

Next, you will need the following parts to build up the frame for the wheels:

- Two blue connector pins
- Four black connector pins
- Three black *11L* beams

The required pieces can be seen in the following image:

Figure 5.7 – Building leverage for leveled height of robot

You will build a bit of a base to level the scorpion build. To do this, start by adding the two blue connector pins to one of the black *11L* beams into the third pin hole on either side. Connect another black beam and add one black connector pin to this second beam. Lastly, add another black beam with another three black connector pins (see *Figure 5.7* for the placement of black connector pins). This stack of three beams will connect to the wheel build you just completed, as illustrated in the following image:

Figure 5.8 – Wheels and leveler piece together

This part will be added to the teal base plate at the edge of the piece, as follows:

Figure 5.9 – Back wheels added to teal plate

Let's now add the motors. You will need the following pieces:

- Two motors
- Ten black connector pins
- Two black rubber tire wheels
- Four gray connector pins with bushings

First, attach the wheels to each of the motors using two gray connector pins with bushings. Proceed to add five black connector pins to each of the motors, placing four pins by the wheels and one to the inside pin hole on the back, as illustrated in the following image:

Figure 5.10 – Preparing the motors

You will add the motors to the opposite side of where you added the wheel build on the teal base plate, as illustrated in the following image:

Figure 5.11 – Motors and wheels added to base plate

Flip this over to ensure your build is level and that everything is securely connected. It should look like this:

Figure 5.12 – Base plate should be level

For the next part, you will need the following pieces:

- One Intelligent Hub

- Four black connector pins

- Two wire connectors

Add four black connector pins to the underside of the Intelligent Hub, as follows:

Figure 5.13 – Intelligent Hub prep

Attach the Intelligent Hub to the teal base plate. You will add the Intelligent Hub to the third pin hole from the end of the teal base plate, opposite where the wheels are attached. Once you do that, go ahead and secure the wires so that they are not sticking out. The result should look like this:

Figure 5.14 – Intelligent Hub added along with wire clips

From the other angle, you should have a nice tight-looking build up until this point. You can see what it looks like from the back to see how the wires can be tucked away, as illustrated in the following image:

Figure 5.15 – Back view of the robot

The base is now complete and the main body is ready to move. It is now time to add the next parts to our scorpion.

Building the tail

Our next step is to add motors three and four to the sides. You are going to use two motors for an equal balance of the body. This will also allow the tail to be strongly held to the body of the robot.

To get started, you will need the following pieces:

- Two motors
- Four black connector pins
- Two white perpendicular connector pins
- Four wire clips
- Two blue connector pins
- Two black *11L* beams
- One distance sensor
- Two black round elbow connectors
- Four blue axle pins

Using two black connector pins for each motor, attach the motors to the sides of the teal base plate, as follows:

Figure 5.16 – Side motors for the tail

Next, insert a white perpendicular connector pin to each of the motors on the top of each motor on the edge, as follows:

Figure 5.17 – White connector pin added to top of each motor

This is also a great time to use the wire clips to organize your wires. Later on, this might be a bit tricky to go back and do. Organization early on is always important, especially as you work in some tight spaces. The wire clips can be seen in the following image:

Figure 5.18 – Using the wire clips to help with wire management

This is also a good time to connect both of your motors to your Intelligent Hub. You will want to plug your motors to the following ports:

- Tail motors motors are plugged into ports **A** and **E**
- Wheel motors are plugged into ports **B** (left wheel) and **F** (right wheel)

You can see a side view of the build here:

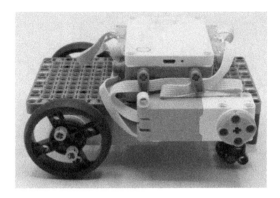

Figure 5.19 – Side view of robot build

Finally, you will extend the back side with two beams to allow proper room for the distance sensor to be added to the back. Use the two blue connector pins to attach the two black *11L* beams to the back of the robot, as illustrated in the following image:

Figure 5.20 – Black beams to extend the back of robot

Once you have the blue connector pins inserted on the two black beams, go ahead and add them to the back of the teal base plate. They will stand out a bit at the back at this point, but it will all come together in later steps.

At this point, your build should look like this:

Figure 5.21 – Black beams added for the sensor

You now add the distance sensor to detect any movement from behind, using the black round elbow connectors to secure the back of the sensor. The black round elbow connectors will attach to the teal base plate, using two blue axle pins. You will plug this sensor into port **C**. The result should look like this:

Figure 5.22 – Sensor attached with black elbow connector pins

Here is what the back of the robot should look like at this point in time:

Figure 5.23 – Sensor added to the teal base plate and rest on black beams

Now that you have the distance sensors added and the base of the robot is all assembled, let's proceed with adding the color sensor to help the scorpion robot respond to its environment.

Connecting the color sensor

Let's head to the front of the scorpion and get our color sensor in place. This sensor will detect any creature that moves too close to the scorpion and will be dealt an attack with the deadly stinger.

You will notice that you are securing both sensors (distance and color) with the black, round, 90-degree elbow pieces to attach from behind, giving us space on the sides to expand our builds later.

You will need the following pieces:

- Two black round elbow connectors
- Four blue axle pins
- One color sensor
- Two teal *3L* beams
- One teal *9L* beam
- Six black connector pins

The required pieces can be seen in the following image:

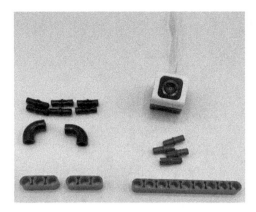

Figure 5.24 – Layout of parts

To begin this section, add the blue axle pins to the black round elbow connectors, as illustrated in the following image:

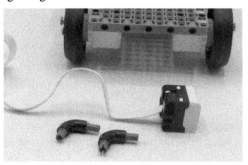

Figure 5.25 – Prep for the color sensor

Attach these to the back of the color sensor and then attach the color sensor to the front of the robot build, as follows:

Figure 5.26 – Color sensor attached using black round elbow connector

Prep your teal beams. Add two black connector pins to each of the teal *3L* beams. Add two more pins to the ends of the *9L* teal beam.

The result can be seen in the following image:

Figure 5.27 – Parts to secure the color sensor

Install one of the *3L* beam to either side of the color sensor to help hold it in place. Add the *9L* beam to the front of the teal base plate. You will also plug the color sensor into port **D**.

The result should look like this:

Figure 5.28 – 3L beams added to sides of color sensor

Once the sensors are in place, it's now time to begin to bring the scorpion to life. To do this, you will need the following pieces:

- Two gray connector perpendicular pins
- Two teal *3L* beams

- Eight black connector pins
- Three black *5x7* open frames
- Two black *3x5 L* beams

Take two of the black *5x7* open frames. On one of the *7L* sides, add a gray connector perpendicular pin. On the gray connector pin, attach a teal *3L* beam. Finally, add a black connector pin to the middle pin hole of the teal *3L* beam.

The result should look like this:

Figure 5.29 – Open frame prep and setup

Add each of these parts to both sides of the color sensor. Remember that there is already a teal *3L* beam attached to either side of the color sensor. Add this part on top of that teal beam, as follows:

Figure 5.30 – Open frames added to top of 3L beam

Locate your third *5x7* black open frame and add four black connector pins to each of the four corners, as illustrated in the following image:

Figure 5.31 – Open frame for the front of the robot

Install this piece on the front of the robot. This will serve as a structure around the color sensor and will also secure the two open frames sitting on top of it.

The result should look like this:

Figure 5.32 – Open center frames joining the other two open frames

The last part to this section of the robot is to add the two *3x5 L* beams to the bottom of the front of the robot. Connect each one to the side of the open frame using a black connector pin, as illustrated in the following image:

Figure 5.33 – Front view of robot at this point of the build

You now have the color sensor installed, but at this point it is not functional. You need to add some triggers to help the color sensor trigger commands in the code, so in the next part, you will build and install the color sensor triggers for your robot.

Adding the color sensor detection triggers

Now that you have installed the sensors, you have to find a way to activate the scorpion as it would act and behave when feeling threatened. In this build, you will use red and yellow *3L* beams to create a trigger in our code so that when something bumps into the scorpion from the front, it will go into attack mode by lunging its tail forward toward the enemy. Through the use of pins and rubber bands, you can create a trigger mechanism that will push the red and yellow pieces forward to activate the color sensor.

When nothing is pressing on these elements, the rubber bands will pull them back to their original starting position.

You will need the following pieces:

- Two yellow *3L* beams
- Two red *3L* beams
- Two black *3x7* angular beams
- Two blue connector pins
- Two tan axle pins
- Two gray axle pins

- Two gray bush stops
- Two gray connector pins with bush stops

In the following screenshot, you can see how to build two of these triggers. Both will be built the same way but with the bush stops being on the outside of the black *3x7* angular beam.

The red beams will go on the left side (if the robot is facing you, it will be on your left) and the yellow beams to your right.

To build this these triggerstrigger mechanism, start with a *3x7* angular black beam. To the inside of the beam, connect the *3L* beams using a blue connector pin and gray axle pin. On the outside, add a tan axle pin and attach the bush stop to the axle side of that pin.

The result can be seen in the following image:

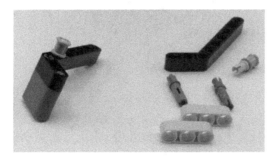

Figure 5.34 – Layout for color sensor triggers

When both parts are built, you should have the following:

Figure 5.35 – Completed sensor triggers

Attach each of these parts using the gray connector pins with bush stops by connecting to the underside of the corner of the open frames. These triggers will activate the color sensor when pushed into the view of the color sensor.

Your build should now look like this:

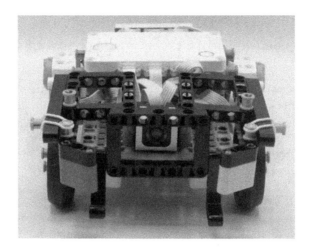

Figure 5.36 – Triggers added to the robot

A key detail to this part of the build process lies within the build component that contains the yellow and red elements. When you attach these parts to the open frames with the gray pins with bush stops, you will connect the triggers from the corner of the open frame and the third hole on the *3x7* angular beam.

It is now time to expand your use of the elements to build out the claws. These claws don't move, but what they do is capture whatever is in the path of the scorpion and force it toward the center. As your scorpion moves forward, the claws funnel the creature to the triggers awaiting the attack!

Before you build the claws, let's finish up the trigger part of this build by adding the rubber bands and a few additional parts.

You will need the following pieces:

- Two white rubber bands
- Six black connector pins
- Two black *11L* beams
- Two blue axle pins
- Two gray bush stops

Begin by adding three black connector pins to each of the black *11L* beams, as illustrated in the following image:

Figure 5.37 – Beams to add to the open frames

Attach both of these to the sides of the open frames, as follows:

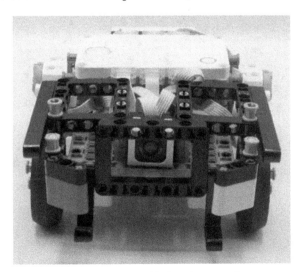

Figure 5.38 – Beams added to the open frames

Check the alignment of your beams just added to the side. The next image provides a side view to help you check better:

Figure 5.39 – Side view of the robot

On each side, add a blue axle pin with a bush stop added to the axle side of the pin. Install this piece on the third pin hole from the end of the black *11L* beam, as illustrated in the following image:

Figure 5.40 – Bush stop added to side for the rubber bands to wrap around

Take your two rubber bands and stretch them around the gray bush stop you just added to the side and to the other bush stop on top of the color sensor trigger, as illustrated in the following image:

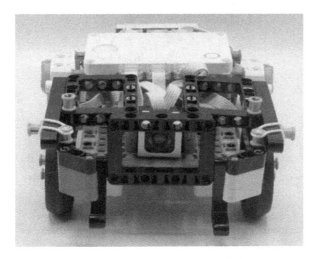

Figure 5.41 – Rubber bands added for triggers for color sensor

You should be able to press the triggers toward the color sensor, and when you let go they should pop back to their original position.

You can continue on to build the claws now that the trigger elements are working.

Building the scorpion claws

You will need the following pieces:

- Two black double-bent beams
- Two black round elbow connectors
- Four blue axle pins

Start with the two black round elbow connectors. Add a blue axle pin to both sides of each of the black round elbow connectors. Add one of each to the black double-bent beams on the second hole of the long part of the beam, as illustrated in the following image:

Figure 5.42 – Building out the first part of the claws

Each of these will then connect to the *11L* black beam on the sides of the robot using the fourth pin hole.

Next, locate the following parts:

- Two black double-bent beams
- Six blue axle connector pins
- Two white axle connectors
- Two black 90-degree axle pins
- Two black connector pins
- Two black *3L* beams

Again, you will build two of the same parts for each side of the robot. Begin by adding a blue connector pin to the pin hole right before the first bend of the black beam. On the opposite side of the beam, add one of the 90-degree axle pins to the end of the beam. Slide on a white connector and then add a blue connector pin to the other end of the white connector, as illustrated in the following image:

Figure 5.43 – Build for second frame of the claws

These two pieces will attach to the very last pin hole of the *11L* beam on the robot. This will connect to the previous black double-bent beam using a blue connector pin, as illustrated in the following image:

Figure 5.44 – Pins for the claws

On the end of the double-bent beam you just installed, add a blue axle connector pin and black connector pin. Then, attach a *3L* black beam to each of the ends.

The result should look like this:

Figure 5.45 – 3L beams added to pins

Finally, you need to build the claws. You will need the following pieces:

- Four small white angled panels
- Two black *3L* beams
- Four black connector pins
- Two blue connector pins
- Two white connector pins with pin hole

Let's continue by starting with the blue connector pins. Add each blue pin through the white connector pin. Use this piece to then attach the two white angled panels on either side to build the look of the claw. Next, secure these pieces in place using a black *3L* beam and two black connector pins to hold them in place.

You will build two of these claws. They should look like this:

Figure 5.46 – Claw builds

Each of these claws will then be added to the pin hole on the *3L* black beam that is on the end of each of the robot arms, as illustrated in the following image:

Figure 5.47 – Claws added to robot

This is how the claws look from the top:

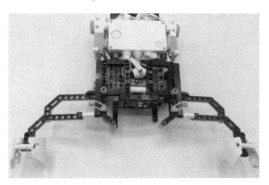

Figure 5.48 – Top view of the claws

Before moving on to the next step, ensure your pins are strong and that the elements are in a good sound structure. You might need to check that your pins are properly secured. The claws will have some movement based on the design but should not fall off or break with some contact.

Building the scorpion's exoskeleton

You will now use many of the white elements typically used for vehicles and robot body designs to create the look of a scorpion. Additionally, these pieces help secure the build and hide wires underneath to give the build a sleeker look. You will notice there are some wire clips used on the sides of the Intelligent Hub, so be sure to use these as you build to hide as much of the wire as you can.

You will now finish up the frame of the robot by adding the head and some structural elements before moving into the final details of the build.

You will need the following pieces:

- One white *13L* beam
- Eight black connector pins
- Two white panels
- Four white pins with friction ridges
- One curved white panel

- One small curved white panel
- Two gray connector pins with bush stops
- Two red axle pins
- Two teal round axle connectors

Begin by adding a black connector pin to each end of the *13L* beam. Attach this piece to the open frames on the top of the robot. This will provide additional support and help to build out the exoskeleton of the scorpion.

The result should look like this:

Figure 5.49 – White beams provide structure to open frames

Next, add a white pin with friction ridges piece to either side of the white panel piece using black connector pins, as illustrated in the following image:

Figure 5.50 – White panel prep

This piece will then be added to the top of the robot body. Using the white pins, you will connect to the open frame and have it line up with the *13L* white beam you just added in the previous step, as illustrated in the following image:

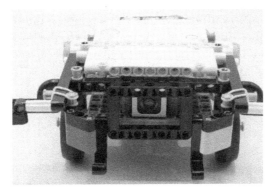

Figure 5.51 – White panel on top of robot

Next, add a white connector pin to either side of your small white curved panel piece using black connector pins, as follows:

Figure 5.52 – Small curved panel to be added for the exoskeleton

This piece will be installed on the robot on top of the open frame that sits at the front of the robot. You will connect it using the white pins and installing it onto the white panel piece you just added in the previous step.

The result should look like this:

Figure 5.53 – White panel on top of open frame

Next, add a gray connector pin with bush stops to the holes on the small curved white panel at the front of the robot. Insert a red axle connector to the bush stop of the gray connector pin. Add a round teal axle connector to give a look of scorpion's eyes, as illustrated in the following image:

Figure 5.54 – Scorpion eyes

Here is a side view of the robot at this point in the build:

Figure 5.55 – Side view of exoskeleton

Looking at the side of the robot, you will now use two black connector pins to add another white panel to the curved white panel that has the eyes installed, as illustrated in the following image:

Figure 5.56 – Another white panel added behind the curved panel

Using two more black connector pins, add another curved white panel to smooth the build down to the Intelligent Hub, as illustrated in the following image:

Figure 5.57 – White panels in place for exoskeleton

The body of the scorpion is now complete with an exoskeleton. You now need to move into the key feature of the scorpion: the tail. Let's get to the tail build so that we can protect our robot!

Designing the tail

To design the tail, we will have to build a frame first around the distance sensor. This frame will help stabilize the tail that you are about to build. As your scorpion attacks, moves, swings, and seeks out prey, you need to make sure the tail does not drop low and trigger your distance sensor, or else you will have one strange-acting animal!

Adding this frame is a perfect fit that still does not take away from the body while providing support and helping the tail stay in place.

To build the frame, you will need the following pieces:

- One black *7x11* open frame
- Four black connector pins
- Two teal *3x5 L* beams
- 2 gray connector pins with bush stops

Begin this build component by adding the *3x5* teal beams to the inside of the open frame using the black connector pins, as illustrated in the following image:

Figure 5.58 – Open frame with teal L beams

Add this piece by connecting the *3x5 L* beams to the pin hole on the side of the distance sensor and using the gray connector pins with bush stops on the front, as illustrated in the following image:

Figure 5.59 – Adding open frame around distance sensor

Let's build the tail. To do this, you will need the following pieces:

- Two curved white panels
- Nine black connector pins
- Two medium-angled white panels
- Three blue connector pins
- One blue axle pin
- One teal *2x4 L* beam

- One teal *5L* beam
- One black *7L* beam
- One white 13L beam

Start by adding two black connector pins to one end of the two curved white panels, as follows:

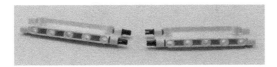

Figure 5.60 – Beginning parts of the tail

On each of the curved panels, Attach the medium-angled white panels to each of the curved panels, as follows:

Figure 5.61 – Extending the tail with white angled panels

With both pieces facing each other, add a white *13L* beam between them and connect them together using three blue connector pins, one blue axle pin, and one black connector pin, as illustrated in the following image:

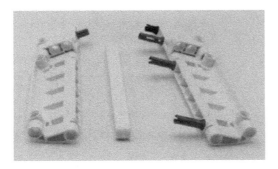

Figure 5.62 – White beam to connect white panels

At the top of the piece, add one teal *2x4 L* beam, as follows:

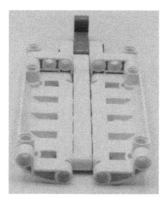

Figure 5.63 – Teal 2x4 L beam serves as the stinger

Hold this build together using a teal *5L* beam and two black connector pins. Add two more black connector pins to the white curved panels. Add a black *7L* beam connected to those black pins.

The result should look like this:

Figure 5.64 – Black beam to secure tail

Locate the following pieces to build the attachment to connect the tail to the scorpion body:

- Fourteen black connector pins
- Two blue axle connectors
- Two teal axle connectors with two pin holes
- Three teal *9L* beams

- Two teal *5L* beams
- Two teal *3x5 L* beams
- Two teal *3L* beams
- Four blue connector pins

Start this part of the tail by adding two black connector pins at one end of two teal *9L* beams, as illustrated in the following image:

Figure 5.65 – Teal beams to build tail connection to motors

Attach both of these pieces to the black beam on the tail, as illustrated in the following image:

Figure 5.66 – Teal beams added to tail

Secure these pieces in place using another teal *9L* beam and two black connector pins, as illustrated in the following image:

Figure 5.67– Another teal beam to secure the other beams

Add two black connector pins to each pin hole of the teal axle connector with two pin holes and add a blue axle connector to the axle hole, as illustrated in the following image:

Figure 5.68 – Prep for the tail attachment

Add these parts you just put together in *Figure 5.68* to the ends of the teal beams and then attach a teal *5L* beam to each end, as illustrated in the following image:

Figure 5.69 – Adding the teal 5L beams

Using four more black connector pins, add two of them to each of the *3x5 L* beams. Add these pieces to the *5L* teal beam. Next, add two blue connector pins to the two *3L* teal beams.

The result should look like this:

Figure 5.70 – Attaching L beams and the prep for 3L beams

The final aspect of the tail is to build a system of elements that you can attach to the motors on the side of the scorpion. Keeping everything symmetrical is an important aspect of this build. Once it is completed, the tail looks awesome. It almost looks like a mini scorpion itself. Here is another view of the tail:

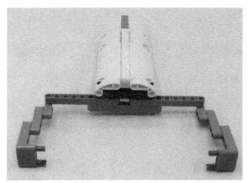

Figure 5.71 – Final view of the tail before adding to the motors

Now, it's time to attach the tail to the two motors. Check to make sure everything is secure and clicked into place. Once you have everything secured, it's time to write some code to make this scorpion come to life.

This is how the tail looks from behind:

Figure 5.72 – Rear view of the tail when raised

Check that the tail moves up and down by gently moving it up and down with your hand. Your scorpion should now look like a scorpion. Check out the following image for a top view of the body:

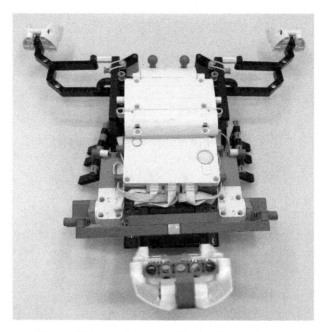

Figure 5.73 – Aerial view of the build with the tail

You have now completed the build. You now have one incredible-looking scorpion. Let's head over to the coding platform to bring our scorpion to life. You will build two coding programs: one for self-control using the app, and an autonomous program.

Writing the code

You will be writing two programs for this build. The first program will allow the robot to move autonomously without any help from its human companion. The second program will be a program that will allow you to control the robot using the remote-control feature of the app.

Connecting sensors and motors to the ports

Before we get into the programming, let's make sure all motors and sensors are properly plugged into the Intelligent Hub. The two motors for the tail should be plugged into ports **A** and **E**. The two-wheel motors will be plugged into ports **B** and **F**. The left wheel will be in port **B** and the right wheel will be plugged into port **F**.

For the sensors, you will plug the distance sensor into port **C**. Finally, the color sensor will plug into port **D**.

Check all connections using the **Port** View in the software.

This view is reproduced here:

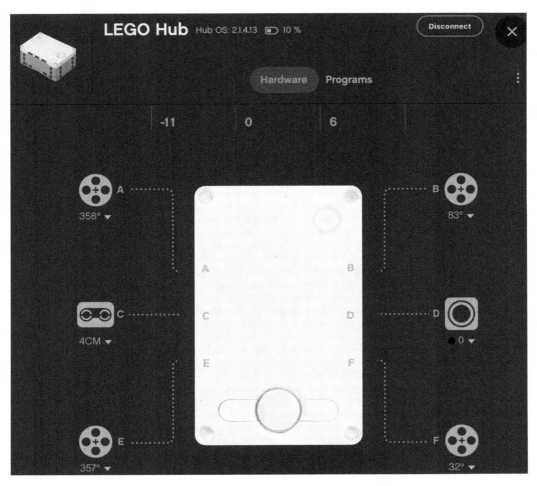

Figure 5.74 – Port View in the MINDSTORMS software

Now that you have all your motors and sensors properly plugged in, let's begin the coding journey to bring your scorpion to life.

Writing an autonomous robot program

This section is going to walk through the steps to write a program that will allow your scorpion to operate on its own using sensors and motors. The following steps will show you how to write this code:

1. Open up the MINDSTORMS software.
2. Click on **Projects** at the bottom of the menu bar.
3. Scroll down to **Other** and click on **Create New Project**.
4. Choose to make a **Word Blocks** program., as illustrated in the following screenshot:

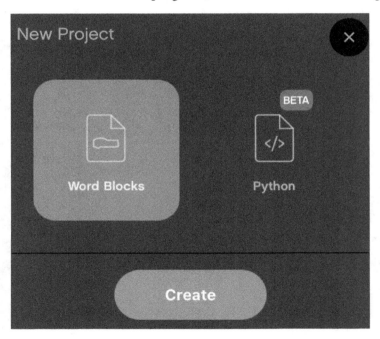

Figure 5.75 – Choosing Word Blocks option

Once you select **Word Blocks**, you should now see the coding canvas begin to add your coding blocks. This is illustrated in the following screenshot:

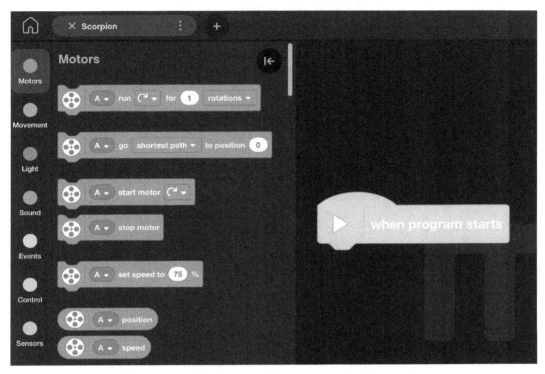

Figure 5.76 – Here is our coding screen once you are ready

5.   Under the **Events** block, when when the program starts, you want to turn on some lights on the robot, just to give you a foundation as you build out the code. You will head to the purple section for light commands and turn on the distance sensor lights along with the *5x5* pixels on the Intelligent Hub. You will use blue so that you can use other colors later to indicate an alarmed or triggered state for the scorpion.

In this sample code, a pixel version of a scorpion has been designed, but you can design any pattern you wish.

Here is the code to activate the lights:

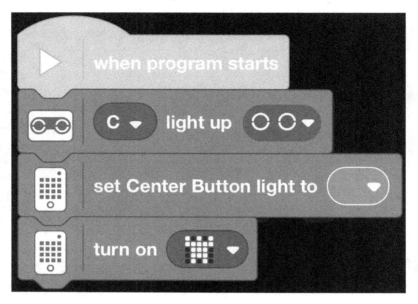

Figure 5.77 – Code to activate lights!

6. The next step is to program the robot to react when the distance sensor detects an object in close proximity. To do this, you will start with a block from the **Events** section and bring over the distance sensor block. Then, you will adjust the proximity. In this example, we use the **%** option of **15%**, but you can adjust this to your liking or use centimeters or inches if you would rather use a specific distance.

7. With this block, you can then decide what you want to happen when an object gets too close to the back of our scorpion. You will use the pink **Movement** blocks to create an action of the scorpion quickly spinning around to face the object.

8. You will need to set the movement motors to the wheels on ports **F** and **B**, then decide on the speed of the motors, and finally move to the right for 1.25 rotations to have the scorpion face the object.

> **Important note**
> Note that you will have to make subtle adjustments based on the speed of your motors, in addition to the surface you have the robot placed on.

9. Following this command of spinning around, you need to have the scorpion move to a strike pose. You will use the tan **Control** blocks to create a repeat set of actions. The **Movement** blocks will activate the tail to strike twice by striking forward and backward twice before ending the loop and kicking out of this entire segment of code.

The process is illustrated in the following screenshot:

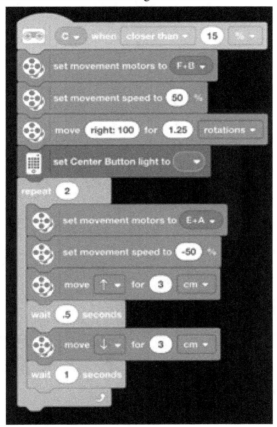

Figure 5.78 – Creating a behavior based on distance sensor sensing alarm

10. Your next step is to write code for when the color sensor is triggered. You will actually write the code for one color and simply duplicate the code and change to the other color. Let's start by using the color sensor block from the **Events** section of the blocks. Choose the correct port **D** and choose the red color. When the color sensor sees red, you then need to move the scorpion to alert mode. Add a light block, changing the pixels from blue to red to indicate danger!

The process is illustrated in the following screenshot:

Figure 5.79 – Color sensor activated seeing red

11. After that, you will create another loop, just like you did in the distance sensor part of the code. You can right-click on the **repeat** block and choose **duplicate**. Drag those blocks over to this segment of code.

The process is illustrated in the following screenshot:

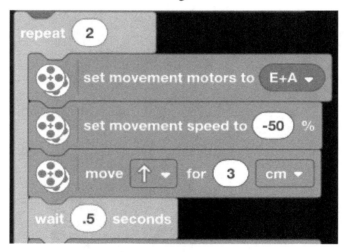

Figure 5.80 – Loop block

12. You will need to add one more section of code to make the scorpion retreat. Scorpions ideally don't like to be bothered even if they sting, so you will have to make the scorpion move backward and await the next sense of danger.

The process is illustrated in the following screenshot:

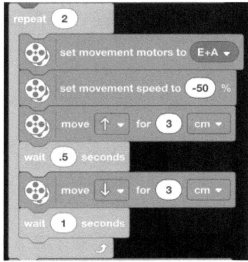

Figure 5.81 – Retreat blocks added

13. You will add some **Movement** blocks after the repeat segment. You need to assign the proper motors, dial in the speed, and then have the motors move the scorpion backward. In the build design of this robot, you have the motors programmed in a backward fashion, so you will program the motors forward to achieve a backward movement.

The process is illustrated in the following screenshot:

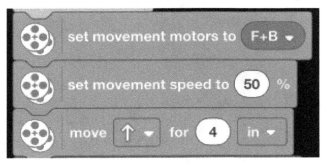

Figure 5.82 – Reset scorpion back to normal state

14. Next, you will change the light back to blue to await the next sense of danger, as illustrated in the following screenshot:

Figure 5.83 – Reset color back to blue

15. Finally, you will duplicate this whole section of code and change from red to yellow so that either color detection will activate these actions, as illustrated in the following screenshot:

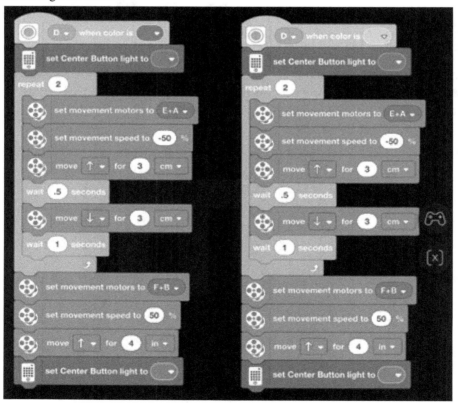

Figure 5.84 – Strike color sensor activated

The following screenshot shows the entire code. The nice thing about this code is the opportunity to code the scorpion to behave as you wish, so have fun editing and remixing the actions to your own liking:

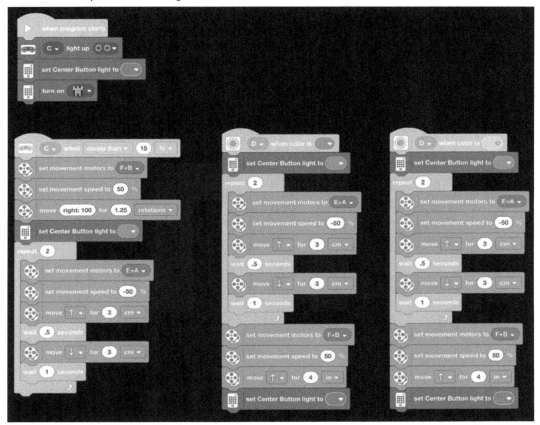

Figure 5.85 – Complete view of the program in MINDSTORMS software

You have just completed one program where the scorpion operates on its own using sensors. Let's take a look at another way of programming the scorpion, using the remote-control feature of the app.

Writing a remote-control program

Additionally, you can write a program where you can use your phone or tablet to control the scorpion yourself. The following steps will show you how to write this code:

1. Open up the MINDSTORMS software.

2. Click on **Projects** at the bottom of the menu bar.

3. Scroll down to **Other** and click on **Create New Project**.

4. Choose to make a **Word Blocks** program., as illustrated in the following screenshot:

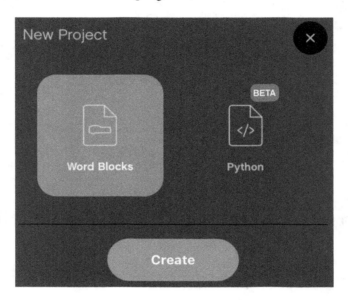

Figure 5.86 – Choosing Word Blocks option

5. Before you can activate the **Remote Controller** blocks, you have to turn on the commands you need. In order to do this, you must click on the joystick icon on the left of the screen. This will give you the screen needed to build your remote control. Once you are here, then need to select the edit icon, which is the pencil in the upper right-hand corner. This can be seen in the following screenshot:

Figure 5.87 – Choosing the pencil icon to create your controller

6. You need to select the blue plus (+) icon at the bottom of the screen to add the necessary widgets. In this project, you will select two of them: the **Joystick** and **Button** widgets. There is no need to code for the color or distance sensors with this project. Be sure to select the blue check to save your design.

The widgets are shown in the following screenshot:

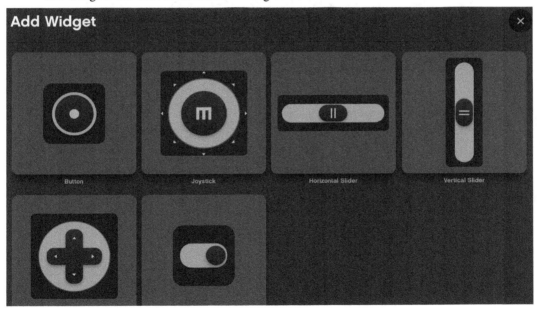

Figure 5.88– Choosing the Joystick and Button widgets

You can also move the widgets around the grid to place them where you would like for your remote controller. Every person has preferences, so adjust this to your needs.

An example layout is shown in the following screenshot:

Figure 5.89 – Controller layout

7. Now that you have the widgets selected, you now have command blocks under the teal **Remote Control** section of code. This code is pretty straightforward. You will have a code block for each direction, so you can essentially code one direction, then duplicate the chunk of code and edit the movement to the proper direction.

8. A key movement to include is when the joystick is released to keep the robot still. If you don't add this option, your robot will continue to move until you turn it off or stop the code entirely.

9. In terms of the button code, you are basically using the same code from the autonomous code outlined earlier to have the tail move back and forth with each button press.

Here is a complete view of the controller program:

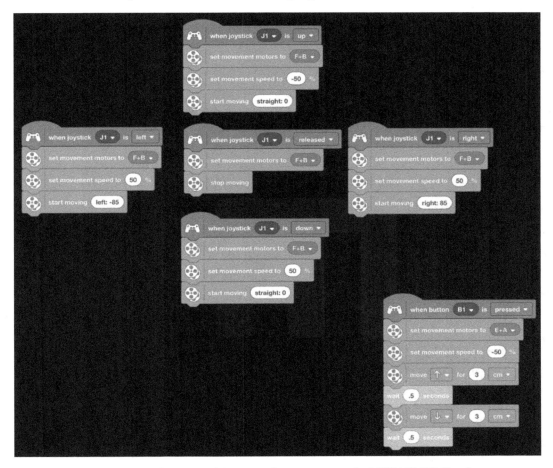

Figure 5.90 – Complete view of the controller program in the MINDSTORMS software

And now, you have a scorpion robot that can work autonomously or with a remote control. The joy now comes from tweaking the design and code to make your own unique style and design. Have fun!

Making it your own

You have been given the framework of an awesome scorpion. How could you add some unique features to make this build even better? How could you possibly combine this with another set of animal features for a super-hybrid creature?

More importantly, how will you tweak the code to have the robot behave differently? What more could be done? You have been given some starter code to have initial success, but your challenge is to take things to the next level! What will you do in a pinch? (Pun intended.)

Here are some ideas to think about to expand on this scorpion build:

- Could you use the color or distance sensor in different ways?

- For movement of the scorpion, could you use the gyro sensor built within the Intelligent Hub?

- Could you explore a scissor mechanism for the tail or limbs?

Summary

In summary, you explored the concept of biomimicry, understanding how incredible animals are by building a scorpion. Aspects of a scorpion have been used in numerous robot builds and designs, from start-up companies to the **National Aeronautics and Space Administration (NASA)**. Understanding how to use sensors to detect motion and movement to activate a strike is a great aspect to your learning. Additionally, showcasing two ways to operate the robot within the software is another nice touch to this kit as you can now think of many new ways to use this robot.

In the next chapter, you will explore a similar type of thinking and design but for a different purpose. You will enter the world of sumobots, making a robot that will battle the best of the best in sumo arenas. Let's go!

6
Building a Solid Sumobot

Sumobots and battlebots are both terms that you may have heard of before. In case you don't know what sumobots are, they are basically robots that are designed to battle one another. Basically, it is a sport where two robots battle in a head-to-head competition to outlast the other robot. Battle robots are a classic build challenge for any robot enthusiast. From the popular YouTube show that led to shows that are now on TV, Twitch, and other platforms, you can find robots battling on all types of arenas, designed from about every conceivable idea you can imagine. These robots come in all shapes and sizes, depending on the rules of the competition. These robot challenges are quite popular in schools, after-school programs, and summer camps when it comes to **sumobots**. The robot you will build in this chapter will provide you with a solid foundation for being dominant in your next arena battle.

Here is a picture of what your base sumobot will look like by the end of this chapter:

Figure 6.1 – Sumobot

In this chapter, you will break down the build and program as follows:

- Preparing the main frame
- Increasing the torque of wheels using gears
- Adding the sensors
- Building the back bumper
- Strengthening the frame with outside supports
- Programming the sumobot to stay in the arena
- Programming the sumobot to attack when the enemy is close

Technical requirements

To build the robot, all you will need is the Robot Inventor Kit. For programming, you will need the LEGO MINDSTORMS app/software.

You can find the code for this chapter at `https://github.com/PacktPublishing/Smart-Robotics-with-LEGO-MINDSTORMS-Robot-Inventor/blob/main/Chapter%206%20Sumobot%20Code.lms`.

If you would like a more detailed photo-by-photo build process of the robot, please head here to view the relevant images: `https://bit.ly/30JaXvB`.

Building the robot

Before we get into building this robot, let's explore the strategy we'll be using. There are a lot of strategies in the world of sumobot competitions, but for the sake of this chapter, you will stick with probably the most tried and tested methods to guarantee sumobot success. The design of this particular sumobot is based on the following strategies:

- The robot should be low to the ground with as little clearance space as possible from the ground to prevent it from being flipped over.
- The robot should be low in terms of height to keep its weight distribution and center of gravity low to the ground.
- Gears should be used to create more torque and power for the robot to push and keep it from being pushed around.

Keeping these three features in mind will help you understand why the robot is designed the way it is. Additionally, the robot has been designed in a way that it allows plenty of customization to be made to it, without us losing sight of these strategies.

Preparing the main frame

For this build, we will use the *11x17* teal plate to keep things sturdy and strong. By using this plate, along with the two large frames, we will begin to design a strong base for the robot to operate on.

To get started, you will need the following pieces:

- One teal *11x17* base plates
- Two black *11x15* open frames
- One black *7x11* open frames
- 19 black connector pins
- Two teal *3x3* Technic pieces
- Two brown *5L* axles with stops
- Four blue connector pins
- Four teal *2x4* L beams

Begin with the base plate, three black connector pins, and two black *11x15* open frames:

Figure 6.2 – Floor of the robot

Bring the two open frames together using three black connector pins:

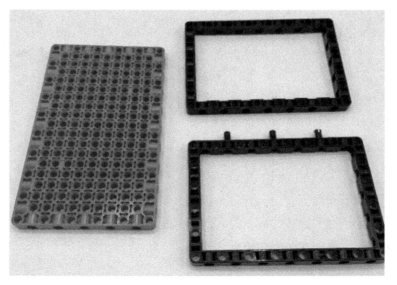

Figure 6.3 – Three black pins to connect the frames

Add another eight black connector pins to the open frames:

Figure 6.4 – Positions of the black connector pins

Using four more black connector pins, place one on each of the two teal *3x3* pieces and two to the teal *11x19* plate:

Figure 6.5 – Teal 3x3 pieces to be added to the base plate

These elements will provide additional support for what will become our back sliders for the robot to maneuver properly:

Figure 6.6 – Teal 3x3 slider supports

Once you have those *3x3* elements connected to the base plate, go ahead and add the open frames to the top of the teal base plate using the eight black connector pins you added to the open frames in the previous steps:

Figure 6.7 – Stack the open frame on the teal base plate

Use four more black connector pins and the two brown *5L* axles and add them to the teal plate and *3x3* Technic pieces:

Figure 6.8 – Brown axles and pins added

Add the black *7x11* open frame to the pins you just installed on the teal plate:

Figure 6.9 – 7x11 open frame added

Next, add four blue connector pins to the open frames:

Figure 6.10 – Blue connector pins added to the open frame

Go ahead and flip over and further secure the bottom by pushing in all the connector pins properly. This will prevent the robot from falling apart upon contact:

Figure 6.11 – Bottom side of robot

Now that your robot is flipped over, add the four teal *2x4 L* beams to the pins that are available:

Figure 6.12 – L beams added to the pins

You should now see the brown axle. Here, you will add your sliders using the following pieces:

- Two smooth black wheels
- Two gray bush stops

These pieces will act as sliders to allow the robot to quickly pivot, spin, and move around the arena:

Figure 6.13 – Slider elements

Add the wheels to the brown axles and secure them in place using the gray bush stops:

Figure 6.14 – Sliders complete

This section is complete. It is now time to add the Intelligent Hub and motors.

Increasing the torque of the robot's wheels using gears

Now that the bottom of the base is nearly complete, let's flip it back over and start adding the motors and Intelligent Hub to bring the robot to life.

To build out the motors and Intelligent Hub, you will need the following:

- One Intelligent Hub
- Two motors
- Two wire clips
- Two gray bush stops
- Two black *8L* axles
- Two black 12-tooth double bevel gears
- Two red axle pins
- 12 black connector pins

To begin, you must push the black axles through the large black open frames. You will install one gray bush stop between the frame and end of the axle for spacing reasons. You must also add the black gears to each motor using the red axle pins:

Figure 6.15 – Motors and Intelligent Hub

Next, install both motors to the outside of the frame using black connector pins. Use four for each motor using the four pin holes on the motor:

Figure 6.16 – Motors added to the base plate

Now, go ahead and add the Intelligent Hub by placing four black connector pins in each of the corners on the underside. Be sure to install the Intelligent Hub with the charger port pointing out to make it easier to charge and plug the Intelligent Hub into your computer:

Figure 6.17 – Intelligent Hub added

Now is a good time to use the wire clips to organize your motor wires:

Figure 6.18 – Wire clips to organize wires

Our end goal with our motors is to create more torque. Remember that this robot's strategy is to create more power than our opponent. You are creating a robot that is gearing down and not gearing up. Torque is a measure of the force that can cause an object to rotate about an axis. In your case, you are gearing down. A small gear is spinning a larger gear, so it will take more spins of the smaller gear so get the larger gear to make one complete rotation.

The opposite is also true. If we were to place a large gear on the motor and then attach it to a smaller gear on the wheel, the robot will go much faster (see *Chapter 7, Building a Dragster*, for this example). The one rotation of the larger gear will cause the smaller gear to spin that much faster based on the ratio of the two gears, thus creating more speed.

For the sake of this robot, think of torque as the strength of the vehicle.

You will need the following parts to make this happen:

- Two large tires with rubber traction
- Four gray bush stops
- Two tan 20-tooth double bevel gears
- Two black round axle connector blocks
- Six black connector pins

The following image is a visual to help us see how the parts will go together:

Figure 6.19 – Gearing pieces

The parts in the preceding image are laid out in the order in which they go onto the black axles of the robot. Follow these steps:

1. Slide on a gray bush stop onto the black axle.
2. Slide on the tan gear. This gear should align with the black gear on the motor.
3. Add two black pins to the black round connector and slide them onto the black axle.
4. Slide the tire onto the axle and connect it to the black round connector with the pins.

5.   Hold everything in place using another gray bush stop.

6.   Repeat this on the other wheel:

Figure 6.20 – Wheels complete

This is a very important time to check that everything is aligned and that the gears are connected. There might be some movement if you test the motors, which you will secure better once you've finished the outside frame of the robot. For now, you can test this robot and ensure it moves around okay. Sometimes, the gears can be a bit tight if you smashed the elements too tight. Run some quick tests to ensure things move properly.

If everything moves okay, then we can finish this section by adding two black connector pins to the Intelligent Hub on the top pin hole:

Figure 6.21 – Connector pins added to the Intelligent Hub

Note that one blue axle pin has been added to the right motor in the previous image. Add one now as you will use a wire clip to keep the wires organized from the sensors that you will eventually add.

Adding the sensors

Most sumo arenas are black with a white line painted along the edge of the circular arena. You will need the color sensor facing down to prevent your robot from driving off the edge and losing. The frame you have makes adding a color sensor very easy to do:

Figure 6.22 – Sumobot arena

You will need the following pieces to add a color sensor:

- One color sensor
- Two teal *3x3* Technic pieces
- Six black connector pins

Begin by adding three connector pins to each of the *3x3* Technic pieces. Add two to the back and one on the side. These pieces will connect to the sensor and then eventually connect to the robot:

Figure 6.23 – Teal pieces to frame the color sensor

Keeping the sensor facing down to the ground so that it can detect the edge of the arena, attach this piece to the front of the frame and Intelligent Hub:

Figure 6.24 – Color sensor added to the front

Next, you must add the distance sensor to the front of the robot, right above the color sensor. You will need to build a mini attachment to make this work.

You will need the following pieces:

- One distance sensor
- One black *11L* beam
- Two black connector pins
- One black *7x11* open frame
- Four gray connector pins with bush stops
- Two dark gray axle connector pins
- Two black round connectors

Begin this attachment by adding two black connector pins to a black *11L* beam. Add them to the third pin hole from each edge:

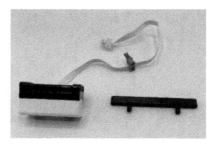

Figure 6.25 – Black beam for sensor support

Add this beam to the back of the distance sensor:

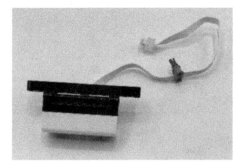

Figure 6.26 – Beam added to the back of the sensor

On each gray connector pin with a bush stop, add a dark gray axle connector pin. On each of the dark gray pins, slide on a black round connector:

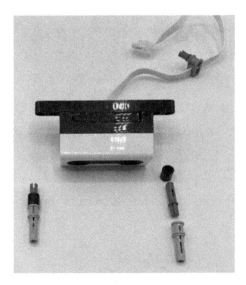

Figure 6.27 – Distant sensor attachment pins

Add these pieces to both ends of the black beam connected to the sensor:

Figure 6.28 – Pins added to the beam

Attach this sensor piece to the *7x11* open frame:

Figure 6.29 – Open frame attached to the pins

Take two more gray connector pins and attach them from the back of the open frame in both of the bottom corners:

Figure 6.30 – Gray pins added to the open frame

This is how the piece should look before you add the remaining components:

Figure 6.31 – Front view of the sensor

Locate the following pieces to build out the front of the distance sensor frame:

- Two black *5x7* open frames
- Two black connector pins
- Two black *7L* beams
- Two blue connector pins

Begin this portion of the build by adding a black connector pin to one of the *5L* sides of the open frames:

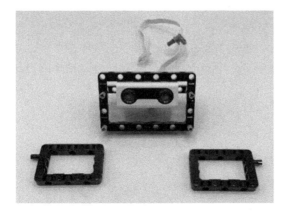

Figure 6.32 – Pins added to the open frames

Attach both these open frames to the pins on the sensor attachment using the gray pins that are available:

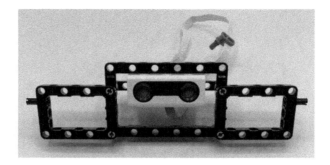

Figure 6.33 – Distance sensor attachment complete

Now that those have been added, let's turn to the beams. Add a blue connector pin to each of the black *7L* beams:

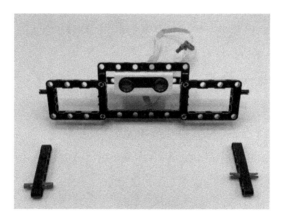

Figure 6.34 – Beams with connector pins

Add a beam to either side of the open frames you just attached to the distance sensor:

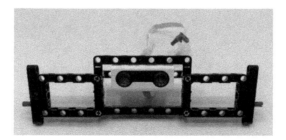

Figure 6.35 – Beams added to the sensor attachment

Finally, you will finish the front of the robot by building out the rest of it. This will help you achieve a square and secure body frame.

You will need the following pieces:

- Eight black connector pins
- Two small curved white panels
- Two medium curved white panels

Begin by adding black connector pins to all the white panel pieces, as shown in the following image:

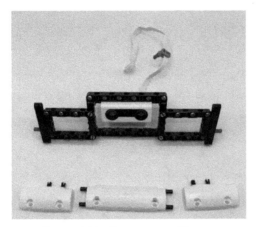

Figure 6.36 – Bumper panel layout

Secure them all together into one piece:

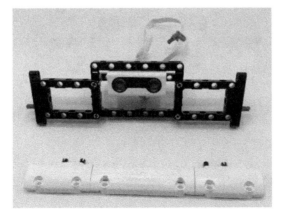

Figure 6.37 – Bumper panel pieces put together

Next, you must add this bumper piece to the front of the robot using the white elements. This will create a mini plow of sorts, which will protect your robot from being flipped. The robot will also be able to use it as a plow to hopefully lift your opponent as you continue to push them backward, out of the arena:

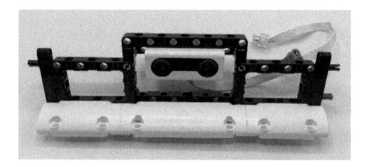

Figure 6.38 – Bumper panel added to the distance sensor frame

At this point, you should have these two parts of your robot built and complete:

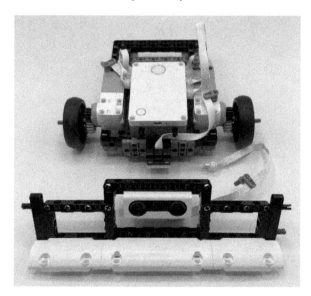

Figure 6.39 – Robot body and distance sensor build

Now, go ahead and connect it to the front of the robot. This front piece goes over the color sensor and keeps it out of view.

Take your time and work your wires toward the Intelligent Hub, ensuring they don't come into contact with the wheels and gears. Also, ensure the wires don't drag on the ground and accidentally slide under the color sensor. Use the wire clips to keep the wires up and out of the way:

Figure 6.40 – Front plow attachment installed

Let's turn the robot around and complete the backside and bumper of the robot now that the front is complete:

Figure 6.41 – Backside of robot

Let's move to the back to build out the back bumper so that our robot is prepared for an attack from either side.

Building the back bumper

You will be creating a similar structure to what we created for the front of the robot, with the exception that there will be no sensors to serve as a plow and bumper.

You will need the following pieces:

- Two black *5x7* open frames
- Two black *2x4 L* beams
- Eight black connector pins

You will start by adding four black connector pins to the *5x7* open frames. On the outside of each frame, attach the *2x4 L* beams, ensuring they're facing up:

Figure 6.42 – Open frames with L beams on the outside

Proceed to add each of the open frames to the larger open frame of the robot itself:

Figure 6.43 – Open frames added to the robot's body

Next, you need to add some structure and support for the robot. To do this, you will need the following:

- Two black *11L* beams
- One teal *5L* beam
- Eight black connector pins

Add these three pieces to the top of the open frames already on the robot. These beams serve as a support structure. Use the black connector pins to hold them all in place:

Figure 6.44 – Beam support for the open frames

Now, you must add the plow bumper to the back. You will need the elements laid out in *Figure 6.45* and assemble them as shown. The back bumper will be less of a plow and more of a protector for if you are attacked from behind by your opponent. The rounded aspect of the white pieces will also serve as a plow that could potentially lift your opponent up.

One detail to pay attention to is the teal *3x3* piece. You will see that you are only using one connector pin on each side instead of two. The spacing of the pin holes doesn't allow for two connector pins on each side, so you will be using one on each side and slightly tilting this piece so that it flows with the white elements.

You will need the following pieces:

- Three teal *9L* beams
- 12 black connector pins
- Two white curved white panels

- One teal *3x3* Technic piece
- Two black *11L* beams
- Two blue connector pins

Here's how these pieces all go together:

1. Start with three teal beams laid out across your workspace.
2. Using three black connector pins, attach the white curved panels to the outside teal beams.
3. Connect these white pieces together using two black connector pins and a teal *3x3* piece between them. The teal piece will be slightly angled.
4. Using a blue connector pin and black connector pin, add a black *11L* beam to the top of each of the white curved panels. Do this on both sides:

Figure 6.45 – Back bumper elements

Here is what this bumper piece will look like when it's been built:

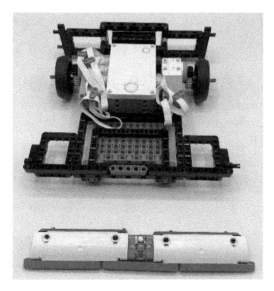

Figure 6.46 – Back bumper complete

Once that bumper has been built, it will connect to the back of the robot and provide a nice layer of protection, keeping another robot from getting underneath your robot. The bumper should be on the ground or very close to it as the wheels move around. Take the time to test your wheels and make sure everything still moves properly. A fine line of spacing is needed to keep everything moving smoothly:

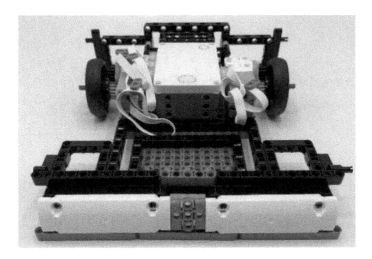

Figure 6.47 – Back bumper attached

There's one last step, and that is to secure the sides and secure the robot so that it has a strong square protection frame. Let's dive into this final step of building.

Strengthening the frame with outside supports

To start, we will create the same side panels. The only difference will be in the color of the *1x5* Technic beams on each side. One side will be all teal, while the other will be all black. You could alternate colors if you wish.

Essentially, you are building two copies of the same build, but the *L* pieces will be on the opposite sides of the *7L* beams.

You will need the following pieces:

- Four black *3x5 L* beams
- 16 black connector pins
- Two white panels
- Six black *5L* beams
- Six teal *5L* beams
- Four black *7L* beams
- 16 blue connector pins

Here's how these pieces all fit together. Use *Figure 6.48* to see the layout of the parts if a visual helps:

1. Add two black *3x5 L* beams to the inside of a white panel using four connector pins.
2. Add a *5L* beam to the white panel using two blue connector pins.
3. Slide another *5L* beam into the blue connector pin.
4. Add four more blue connector pins to another *5L* beam and attach it to the previous beam.
5. Slide two more *5L* beams into the blue connector pins.
6. Add two black connector pins to your last beam and attach it to the five beams that are already connected.
7. Attach another white panel to this beam using two black connector pins.

8.   Using two more blue connector pins, add two *7L* black beams to complete the build:

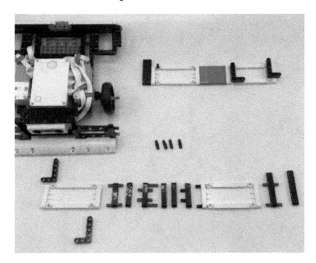

Figure 6.48 – Side panel construction

Here is what your two panel pieces will look like once they've been put together. Note how they are the same builds but have opposite layouts so that you can work on either side of the robot:

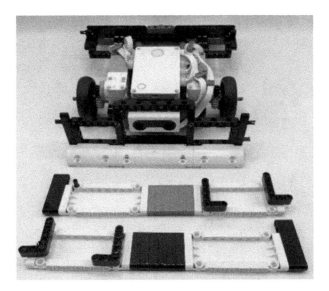

Figure 6.49 – Side panel pieces complete

Looking from a top view, here is how these panel pieces will connect to the sumobot:

Figure 6.50 – Side panels alignment

The panels click and connect to the front and back using the *L* beams that are already on the back bumper and the *7L* beams on the front:

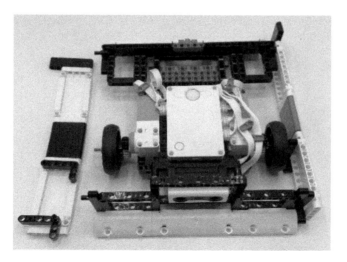

Figure 6.51 – Side panel installed

The one critical detail is the positioning of the axle of the wheels. The axle needs to be placed in the proper hole; otherwise, the robot will have problems moving. Be sure to insert the axle into the second to top hole of the black *3x5 L* beam. This provides proper clearance off the ground and also keeps the tension where it should be, keeping the gears from spinning out or not moving at all:

Figure 6.52 – Wheel axle alignment

Here is how your sumobot should look at this point:

Figure 6.53 – Sumobot build checkpoint

The last step is to finish off the square frame by adding structural support. Using beams, you will secure the sides to the front and back, as well as provide strength all around by adding two layers of beams until everything is balanced out.

You will need the following pieces:

- 17 black connector pins
- One black round connector
- Two black *11L* beams
- Two black *3x5 L* beams
- Two black *15L* beams
- Two black *7L* beams

Begin by adding the black round connector to the middle pin of the teal piece on the back of the sumobot, opposite the distance and color sensors:

Figure 6.54 – Round connector added to the teal beam

Using two black connector pins per beam, attach the *11L* black beams to either side of the round connector:

Figure 6.55 – Black beams added to the sides of the round connector pins

Using two more black connector pins for each black 3x5 *L* beam, add an *L* beam to either side of these beams:

Figure 6.56 – L beams added

Using the *15L* black beams and two black connector pins, add these to the side walls to strengthen the panels:

Figure 6.57 – Beams added to the side panels

Finally, add a black *7L* beam to either side using two more black connector pins to finish up the first layer of support:

Figure 6.58 – 7L beams added to the side panels

Here is the first round of structural support:

Figure 6.59 – First layer of strengthening the frame

You need to add one more layer of support to bring structural support and to smooth everything out. You will need the following pieces:

- Two black *7L* beams
- One black *15L* beam
- Six black connector pins

Begin the second layer by adding six black connector pins across the back:

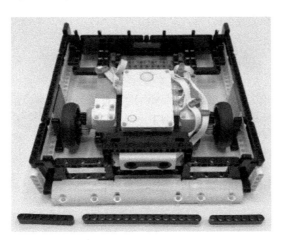

Figure 6.60 – Adding six pins to the beams

Then, add the beams to the pins:

Figure 6.61 – Beams added to the pins

The next step is to add a layer to each side. Due to part constraints, here is what you will need:

- 18 black connector pins
- Two blue axle pins
- Two black *2x4 L* beams
- Two black round connectors
- Two black *15L* beams
- Four black *3L* beams

You will make the same build on either side of the robot supports. You will use the same pieces on either side. Note that the blue axle pin is for the axle hole of the *2x4 L* beam. The rest are all using the black connector pins to hold all the pieces together. The following image showcases how they line up on the sides:

Figure 6.62 – Parts and layout for side panel support

Here is the second layer of black Technic beams:

Figure 6.63 – Second layer of strengthening the frame

Now, you have one awesome sumobot ready to be coded so that you can put it to work in the arena!

Here is the back view of the sumobot:

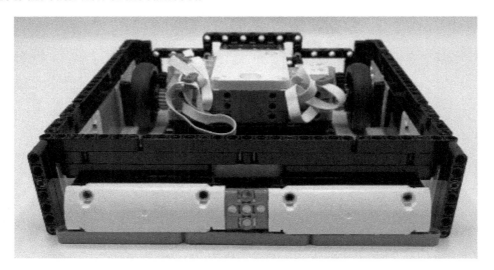

Figure 6.64 – Back view

Here is the front view of the sumobot:

Figure 6.65 – Front view

Here is the side view of the sumobot:

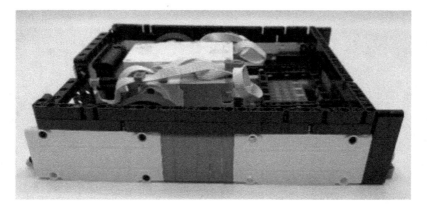

Figure 6.66 – Side view

Whew! You have done it. That's one sharp-looking and effective sumobot. Now, it is time to write some code so that you can compete in the arena.

Writing the code

The code for this project needs to solve a few key issues when it comes to sumobot battles and the strategy we are focusing on. Here are the three main goals of the code that you will be writing:

- The robot needs to stop when it sees white to keep it from driving out of the arena.
- The robot needs to detect when another robot is close so that it can push them forward and drive them out of the arena.
- The robot needs to be steady and consistent to avoid any unnecessary movements that may cause our robot fall out of the arena.

Let's double-check our ports and start writing the code to achieve these goals.

The ports

Before you write your code, it is good to make sure all the motors and sensors are plugged in properly. Using **Port View**, you can double-check the proper ports. The wheel motors will need be plugged into ports **E** and **F**. The distance sensor needs to be plugged into port **A**. The color sensor will need to be plugged into port **C**.

Additionally, you might need to change the settings of the distance sensor to inches and the color sensor to reflect any light if you have any issues with the code later:

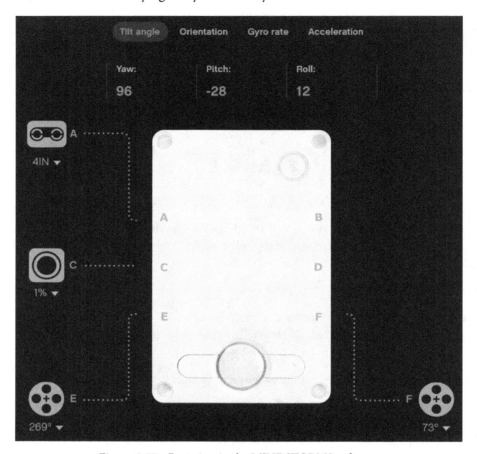

Figure 6.67 – Port view in the MINDSTORMS software

Now that you know everything is plugged in properly, it is time to code.

Sumo robot program

To get started, you need to open the coding platform. Here are the steps in case you need to know how to open a new block coding program:

1. Open the **MINDSTORMS** software.

2. Click on **Projects** at the bottom of the menu bar.

3. Scroll down to **Other** and click on **Create New Project**.

4. Choose to make a **Word Blocks** program.

Main code sequence

The program has three main sections. You will build them step by step. Let's start with this first section of code. You can see it in *Figure 6.68*. The steps to create this code are as follows:

1. Sumobot matches begin with a countdown. You will add a 3-second countdown timer using the purple light blocks. We will display a number each second that will count down 3-2-1. You can design your own numbers, shapes, or symbols. This gives the participant time to back away from the arena before the battle begins:

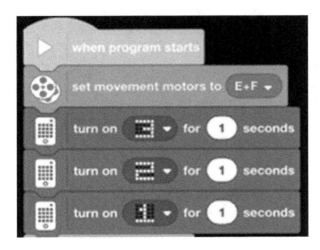

Figure 6.68 – 3-2-1 countdown

2. You will create a variable called Action that will be used to change the conditions of the variable based on sensor inputs. Once you create this variable, go ahead and add a block that sets the action to **option 1** by using the **set variable** block. This can be found in the variable orange coding blocks:

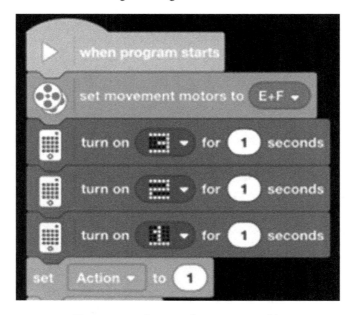

Figure 6.69 – Creating the Action variable

3. Go to the **Control** blocks and drop in a **Forever** block under the **Set Action to 1** block we just added in *step 2*. This **Forever** block will help our robot keep making decisions until we stop the code.

4. In the **Forever** block, you will add four of the same types of code chunks. You will drop in an **If** block with a green operator block to compare the variable to a number. Write this out so that we have four actions numbered 1, 2, 3, and 4.

5. For **Action 1**, you will simply have your robot move forward by adding the **Start Moving** block, which can be found in the pink **More Movement** blocks. Keep the speed low to begin with; you can always go back and adjust it to your liking:

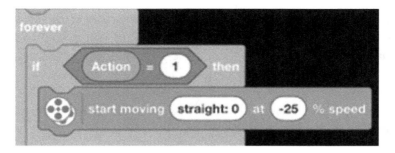

Figure 6.70 – Action 1 decision

6. For **Action 2**, you will write a command for when the color sensor detects the white perimeter. It will back up for two rotations and randomly move in a certain direction before being told to go back to **Action 1** of moving straight. Again, you can dial this into your liking and adjust how you want your robot to respond when it detects the edge, but for now, you will just have the robot move back for two rotations:

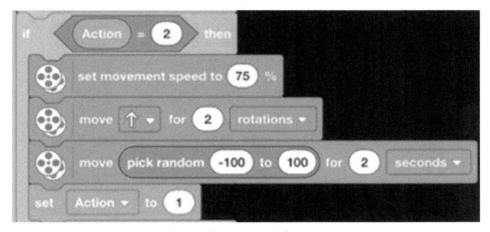

Figure 6.71 – Action 2 decision

7. For **Action 3**, you will write some code that makes the robot move fast and push the other robot forward. This action will be linked to the distant sensor when it detects another robot. A sound has been added to help you audibly know when your robot detects the opponent. This is a useful tip to help refine and make sure your robot is doing what you want it to do. Again, once it pushes forward, it kicks back to **Action 1** to make another decision. It will repeat this step until the sensor no longer detects the opponent:

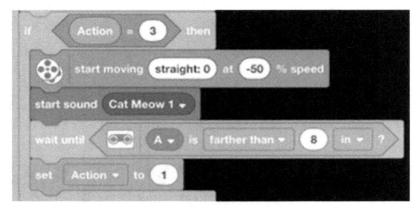

Figure 6.72 – Action 3 decision

8. For **Action 4**, you need the robot to be able to detect an opponent *and* also detect the white perimeter. You don't want to accidentally push yourself off the arena. Again, this will need to be further tweaked to your liking, but for the sake of this example, this code will have the robot back up for one rotation to avoid the edge, reset to **Action 1**, and make another decision:

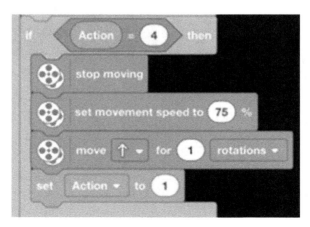

Figure 6.73 – Action 4 decision

Here is what the code looks like once it's completed:

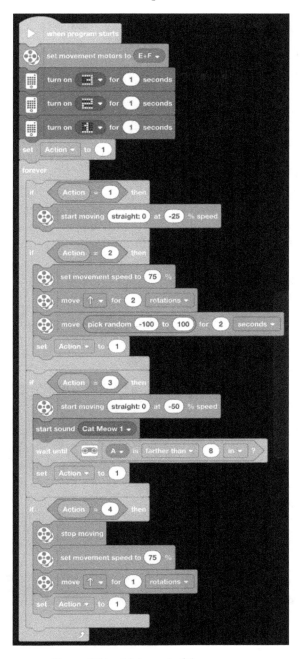

Figure 6.74 – Main part of the program

Double-check your code and if it looks good, then it is time to code the color sensor.

Color sensor code sequence

We need another little chunk of code for the main program to help with decision making. This one focuses on the color sensor. Let's get started:

1. Drop in another yellow **Events** block called **When Program Starts**. You will have several parts of code running at the same time.

2. Insert a **Forever** block into this code.

3. Insert an **If** block so that it's nested in the **Forever** block.

4. Using a sensor block, you will dial in your sensor to the reflection light. You can try using colors that are only black and white, but I have found that these new color sensors are so good that a speck of white dust or chipped paint can activate the sensor. I stick with reflection light, and you can adjust the percentage based on the ambience of the space. To do this, simply place your robot on a black surface and see what percentage reading it provides; then, do the same when it sees a white surface. Change the percentage number on this blue sensor block accordingly.

5. When it detects *white*, add the variable block to change the *action* variable to the number 2. This will activate that sequence of code in the main part of the coding we just completed earlier:

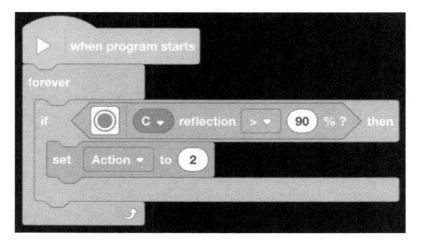

Figure 6.75 – Color sensor program

Double-check your code and if it looks good, you can start programming the distance sensor.

Distance sensor code sequence

You need to write some code for when the distance sensor senses an object within a certain range so that you can deploy an attack strategy. Let's do this now:

1. Drop in another yellow **Events** block called **When Program Starts**. You will have several pieces of code running at the same time.

2. Insert a **Forever** block into this code.

3. Insert an **If** block so that it's nested in the **Forever** block.

4. Using a sensor block, you will dial in your sensor to the distance of your choice. Try different distances to find what works. In my test runs, 6 inches was pretty spot on as that activated when I needed it to at all times, while also not being triggered by objects outside the arena.

5. When it detects an object, add the variable block to change the **Action** variable to the number 3, which will then activate that sequence of code in the main part of the coding we just completed earlier.

6. Insert another **If** block so that it's nested in the **Forever** block and underneath our first **If** block.

7. This **If** block will contain an operator block waiting for *two* variables to trigger the code. In this case, we need the distance sensor *and* the color sensor to be activated. When this happens, our robot will make a fourth decision to prevent itself from falling off the edge while battling a robot.

8. Drop in another **Set Action** block with the condition of 4 to activate that code sequence in our main program:

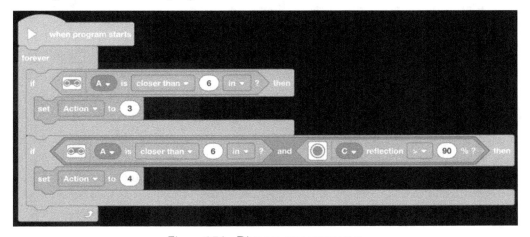

Figure 6.76 – Distance sensor program

In the end, the entire code will look like this:

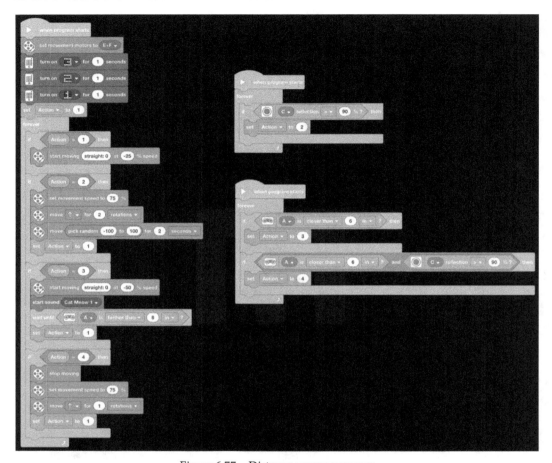

Figure 6.77 – Distance sensor program

And you have done it! You should now have a working sumobot that is full of potential and has places for you to add your own flavor and design ideas. Enjoy!

Make it your own

Now, it is time to hand the robot over to you. This is where you can take what you have built so far and customize the robot to your liking. Plenty of pieces have been left in the bin for you to design aesthetic features and apply new approaches to make your robot more intuitive, and there are plenty of coding options you can utilize to take the robot to the next level.

Here are a few ideas to consider:

- The kit itself is limited in terms of the sensors that can be plugged into the Intelligent Hub. If you have another sensor from another kit or **SPIKE Prime**, then you could add a distance sensor, force sensor, or even a color sensor to the pack to create another decision point in the code so that when the robot senses danger from behind, it can counter. Currently, the robot is dependent on being strong enough to handle an attack from the back to counter and win.

- If you wanted to take a different approach, what if you designed a device that, when the robot is hit from behind, could trigger a *counterattack?*

- Cosmetic appeal. There is plenty of open space at the back and top to fully customize this robot. How can you take the out-of-the-box parts and add some personality to your robot?

Summary

In this chapter, you explored the concepts of gears, sensors, making various decisions based on feedback, and how to use simple engineering principles to build an effective robot. This chapter was focused on providing you with building and coding concepts related to how you can use the different components that are available in the Robot Inventor Kit, as this will help you build a strong sumobot model with high torque and stability via gearing mechanisms. Additionally, you used sensors to trigger the different actions of your sumobot. This ensures that you will have success in battles. You did this by identifying the border of the arena and stopping the sumobot from falling off the edge, as well as using the distance sensor to activate attack mode when your competition is within striking distance.

Now, it is time to engage in a battle. Find a friend, foe, or local competition and see how you do. Feel free to battle other types of robots as well. There are so many ideas, rules, and suggestions online for you to use to explore and expand your sumobot building and strategy deployment. Good luck. There are so many possibilities, so take the time to try new ideas, attachments, sensor placements, and more. In all my years of robotics, sumobots is the one challenge that people love the most. I think you will too!

In the next chapter, you will use gearing again, but for a different purpose: trying to achieve maximum speed. Let's rev our engines and get started by building and racing a dragster!

Building a Dragster

Dragsters that race and are designed for speed are a classic build and one that every builder creates at some point in their lives. I have operated the summer MINDSTORMS Robotics camp for several years and the dragster challenge is a favorite every year that the kids always want to compete in. Whether designing for yourself or competing against others, racing is a blast. In this chapter, we will build a dragster using this kit to see how it turns out in terms of speed and design:

Figure 7.1 – Top view of the dragster you will build in this chapter

In this chapter, we will break down the build and program as follows:

- Building the motor frame
- Adding the wheels with a gear
- Developing the body of the dragster
- Adding the body design
- Programming the dragster to race and capture time

Technical requirements

For the building of the dragster, all you will need is the Robot Inventor Kit. For the programming, you will need the LEGO MINDSTORMS app/software.

Access to the code can be found here: `https://github.com/PacktPublishing/ Smart-Robotics-with-LEGO-MINDSTORMS-Robot-Inventor/blob/main/ Chapter%207%20Dragster%20Code.lms`.

If you would like a more detailed, photo-by-photo build process of the dragster, please head here to view the images: `https://bit.ly/3tlu77b`.

Building the dragster

Before we get into the building of this dragster, let's explore the strategy being used for this dragster. The strategy for drag racing is all about speed – how fast can we get from the starting line to the finish line? That is it! The design of this particular dragster is based on the following strategies:

- Sitting low to the ground to eliminate drag
- Friction points: The less friction we have the better
- Gearing up to max out the speed of the dragster
- Weight balance to help the dragster stay straight

Keeping these features in mind will help you understand why the dragster is built the way it has been designed. Additionally, the dragster has been designed in a way to allow plenty of customization to be done to it without losing sight of these strategies. The body design has been created to give the look of a dragster, but you could easily modify the design to your own liking, as well as adding or reducing weight to the dragster.

In the end, this particular dragster was able to race down a 10-foot long track in 2.7–2.8 seconds.

Building the motor frame

Let's start with the most important feature and function of the dragster, and that is the motor frame. You will be using two motors locked together for the race. We are combining them as we don't need to worry about turns, only going straight and fast! Go ahead and grab two motors to begin the process.

You will need the following pieces:

- Two motors
- One black 36-tooth gear
- One gray *3L* axle
- One black *11x15* open frame
- Two blue connector pins
- Two gray connector pins with bushings
- Two wire clips:

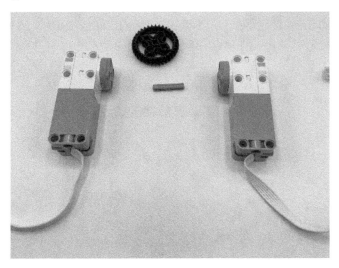

Figure 7.2 – Parts to get started

You will use a gray axle of size *3L* and a black 36-tooth gear to connect the two motors together by placing the gear and axle in between each motor and connecting in the center pin of each motor.

Once you have connected all the components, the combined motors will look like the following:

Figure 7.3 – Axle 3 and a 36-tooth gear to combine the motors

After the motors are joined together, you will place the motors in a *11x15* black open frame. The motors will lock into place using two blue friction pins and two gray connector pins with bushing:

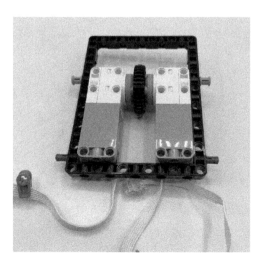

Figure 7.4 – Motors in an open frame

Now that your motors are in place and locked into the *11x15* open frame, you need to add some additional beams to build out the rest of the form to allow the wheels and gear to work properly.

You will need the following:

- Four black *15L* beams
- 14 black pins
- Four teal *3x3* pieces

Place two *15L* beams under the sides of the open frame:

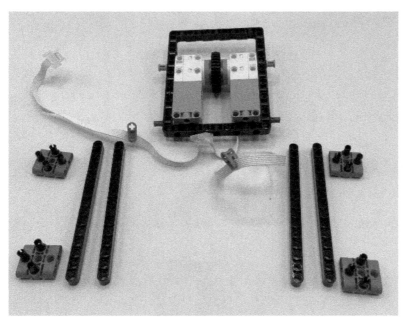

Figure 7.5 – General layout of the part placement

You will connect these to the open frame using the *3x3* teal elements using the black connector pins. Note that the *3x3* teal pieces will only use *three* black connector pins as one pinhole will connect to the blue connector pin we added in the previous step:

Figure 7.6 – Using a teal 3x3 piece to secure the parts in place

For the next step, you will need the following:

- Two gray perpendicular pin connectors with four pins
- Four black pin connectors
- Two teal *2x4* L-shaped beams

Add the gray pin connectors to the top of the motors as seen in the following figure:

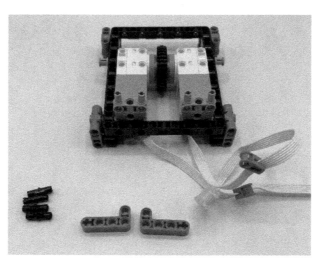

Figure 7.7 – Securing the gray pin connectors in the proper motor location

Use one black pin connector to join the L-shaped beam to the side of the motor and make it flush against the open frame that the motors sit in. Complete this on both motors. Finally, add two black pin connectors to the pinhole available on the gray connector pin on the motor and next to the L-shaped beams:

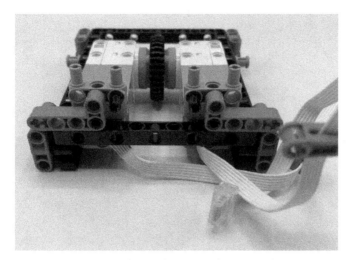

Figure 7.8 – View of the teal L beams in place

You have just finished the frame for the motors. It is time to move on to the next step, adding the wheels to the motors.

Adding the wheels with a gear

For this section, you will be building out the wheels and gearing them up to provide maximum speed.

Here is a list of the parts that you will need:

- One gray axle of size *7L*
- One black 12-tooth gear
- Four white round spacers
- Two white axle connectors

Start with the *7L* gray axle piece. This piece will be the element that will fit through the black *11x15* open frame and allow you to connect the wheels. Additionally, this element helps us to add the small gear to the large gear to gear up our wheels to increase speed:

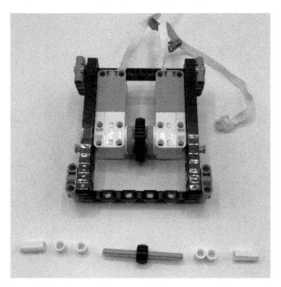

Figure 7.9 – General layout of the parts coming together

Start by taking the 12-tooth gear and centering it on the gray axle piece. On both sides, you will add two white spacers and one axle connector to the ends. Squeeze them all together for a nice tight fit and ensure everything is secure:

Figure 7.10 – This is how the parts look assembled on the axle

Once you have this complete, place this element so that the small gear lines up with the larger gear between the motors and the ends align with the pinholes of the *15L* beams on the sides:

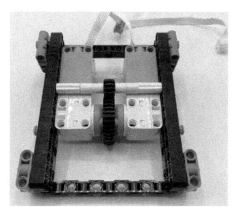

Figure 7.11 – 3x3 teal beams connecting all the parts together

You will now add the wheels to the small gear. You will need the following pieces:

- Two wheels
- Four axle connector block rounds
- Four blue connector pins
- Two red *6L* axles

Push the red *6L* axle through the middle of a wheel. Combine two of the axle connector block rounds together using two of the blue connector pins. Lock these pieces to the inside of the wheel and red axle. Finally, push the red axle through the motor frame, locking into the white axle connector:

Figure 7.12 – Top view of the parts needed

Repeat with the other wheel. Press everything together to make sure things are secure:

Figure 7.13 – Aligning the axles

You have done it! The power of the dragster is ready. Feel free to set this aside as you will now start to build the body of the dragster next.

Developing the body of the dragster

You are going to work backward, starting at the front of the dragster and working toward the motor frame you just built.

To get started, you will need the following elements:

- Two brown *3L* axles with stops
- Two gray bushings
- Two black smooth *18x14* wheels
- Two *3x3* gray perpendicular bent pin connectors
- Two black *5L* beams

Start with the gray perpendicular pin connector piece and add the black *5L* beam to one side. At the end of the beam, slide the brown *3L* axle. On the other side of the black beam, add the wheel and finally the bushing to secure the wheel in place:

Figure 7.14 – One completed part and the other showing the parts needed

Repeat again but flipping the gray perpendicular piece to face the other way:

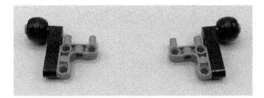

Figure 7.15 – The parts should look and face each other like this

Locate a black *11L* beam and connect the wheels to the ends of the beam. Use the *11L* beam to connect the gray connector pins:

Figure 7.16 – The black beam connects the gray connector pins

Using another black *11L* beam and two black connector pins, secure the wheels on top:

Figure 7.17 – The second black beam with the black connector pins

You should have a part that is strong and stable and looks like the following:

Figure 7.18 – A second black 11L beam placed on top

Next, you will need the following:

- Four blue connector pins
- Two teal round spacers
- One *5x7* black open frame
- One color sensor

Push two blue connectors through the *5L* side of the open frame. Take the other two blue connector pins and slide the teal round spacers on the *2L* pin side:

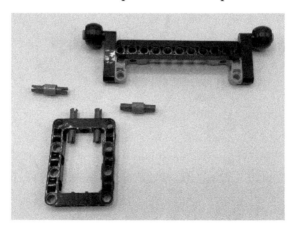

Figure 7.19 – The 2L side of the blue connector goes through the pinhole of the open frame

Add the two blue connector pins to the corner pinholes where you pushed the blue pins through the *5L* side of the open frame:

Figure 7.20 – Be sure to align to the middle of the beam

Clip this piece onto the top and center of the front wheel piece you just built. Once this is locked in, take the color sensor and push it into the blue connector pins on the inner side of the open frame:

Figure 7.21 – Make sure the color sensor is facing down

From here, we will begin to build the body of the dragster. Find the following pieces:

- Two white *5x11* panel pieces
- Two blue connector pins
- Two teal round spacers
- Two black connector pins

Slide the teal round spacers onto the *2L* side of the blue connector pins. Attach these to the topside of the white *5x11* panel. Finally, connect the two black connector pins to the opposite side of the blue connector pins:

Figure 7.22 – White panel layout

Attach this piece to the underside of the black *5x7* open frame of the wheel piece you built in the previous step:

Figure 7.23 – Connecting the white panel to the underside of the open frame

Locate another white *5x11* panel plate and four black connector pins. Connect the white panel plate to the one you just attached to the open frame. Add two black connector pins on both sides:

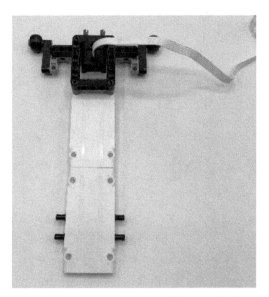

Figure 7.24 – View with the second white panel plate added

Use panel fairing plates that are *6L* in size for each side of the vehicle. Connect them using the black pin connector pieces on the sides of the white panel plates:

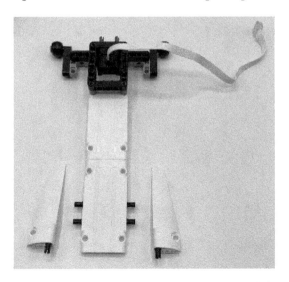

Figure 7.25 – The narrow end of the white piece points toward the color sensor

At this point, you should have these two pieces built:

Figure 7.26 – Double-check you have both parts

These two pieces will join together for the foundation of the dragster frame:

Figure 7.27 – View of the dragster body frame

You are now ready to begin to add some design elements to the body of the dragster. Let's begin.

Adding the body design

You will start this section by flipping the dragster over to the underside. Find the following pieces:

- Four white *13L* beams
- Six blue connector pins

Connect two white *13L* beams and join them with three blue connector pins as shown in the following figure. You will build two of these pieces that will clip into the white panel pieces of the dragster to provide structure and strength to the body of the vehicle:

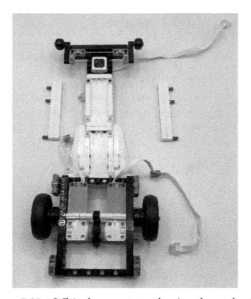

Figure 7.28 – White beams strengthening the underside

Find the following pieces:

- Two teal *2x4* L-shaped beams
- Four black connector pins

Add two black connector pins to the *L*-shaped beams:

Figure 7.29 – Beams and teal L beams connecting to the underside

Connect these pieces to the black open frame and the white beams you just attached to the white panels. The reason for this is to provide one more piece to further strengthen the build of the body. This part helps secure the front of the dragster to the back end of the dragster:

Figure 7.30 – Complete view of the underside

Flip the dragster back over to the regular side. Find four gray perpendicular connector pins and add them to the top of the motors. Two gray connector pin pieces go on each motor. You will be using these to create a frame for the Intelligent Hub to sit on:

Figure 7.31 – Top view of the dragster

For the next part, find these pieces:

- Two teal *9L* beams
- Eight black connector pins
- One black *7x11* open frame
- Two blue axle pin connectors
- The Intelligent Hub

Connect the two teal *9L* beams across the motors on the gray perpendicular connector pieces. Add two black connector pins on each teal *9L* beam in the open pin between where you connected the teal beam onto the motors:

Figure 7.32 – Teal beam to secure the motors

Connect the three blue axle connector pins to the *7x11* open frame. Place the open frame onto the teal *9L* beams using the four black connector pins that you added earlier:

Figure 7.33 – Open frame added to the top

The final step for this part of the dragster is to take the other four black connector pins to the bottom of the Intelligent Hub and lock them into place on top of the open frame:

Figure 7.34 – Securing all the connector pins to the Intelligent Hub

Let's move to the back of the dragster. You will need these pieces:

- One *11x3* white curved panel
- Two white *#2* panel fairings
- Four white 135-degree axle pin connectors
- Two black *12L* axles
- Two teal *3x3* elements
- One white *3x11* panel plate
- Two teal wire clips
- Four blue axle connector pins
- Four black connector pins

Start with the white curved panel and connect it to the backside of the dragster. You should have a friction pin open on the gray perpendicular connector pins that hold the Intelligent Hub. Using the blue axle connector pins, attach the wire clips to the side of the curved panel:

Figure 7.35 – Back view of the dragster

Grab the two white #2 panel fairing pieces and four black connector pins and secure them to the back of the dragster body. This gives some detail to the build, as well as helping secure the open frame to the *3x3* teal pieces:

Figure 7.36 – White fairing elements on top of the 3x3 teal pieces

For the next part, add a blue axle connector pin to the one axle hole of the 135-degree axle connectors. On the other end, insert the black *12L* axle. After you do this, add another 135-degree white axle connector followed by the blue axle pin connectors. Next, you should be able to connect the white panel to the top of this piece using the pinholes. Finally, using two black connector pins on each of the *3x3* teal pieces, connect these to the sides of the white panel.

Add this piece to the back of the dragster. Here is what you should have assembled at this point:

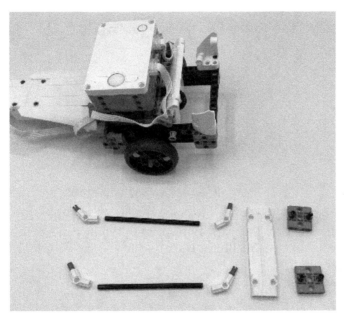

Figure 7.37 – Layout of the back build

Let's build the complete part first. Connect the black axles to the white panel piece using the white connector parts. You will have a build part that should look like the rear end of a dragster race car:

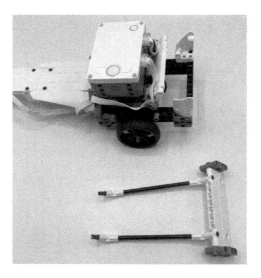

Figure 7.38 – All parts assembled for the back

Now that you have the piece assembled, go ahead and attach it to the body of the dragster on the rear end of the dragster. This part connects to the white panel that was added to the body of the dragster behind the Intelligent Hub. It will begin to really look like a dragster with this piece attached:

Figure 7.39 – Connecting the back piece to the back body of the dragster

It is now time to move back to the front of the dragster body to add some details.

You will need the following parts:

- Four panel fairings (two for the left and two for the right)
- Two smaller panel fairings
- Two black *11L* beams
- 16 black connector pins

This part is pretty straightforward. Using eight black connector pins for each side and three white panel fairing pieces for each side, you will join them together to create an edge piece for both sides of the dragster. As seen in the photos that follow, you will add a black *11L* beam onto the side of the middle white fairing element to then connect to the body of the dragster:

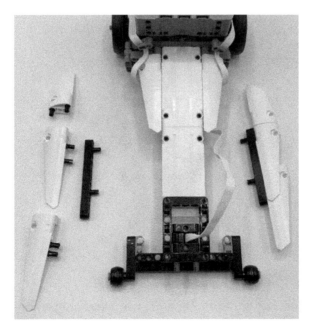

Figure 7.40 – The left side shows the parts needed and the right side shows the completed assembly

You will build two complete pieces, one for the right and one for the left. Once you have them built, go ahead and add them to the sides of the frame of the dragster, as seen in the next figure:

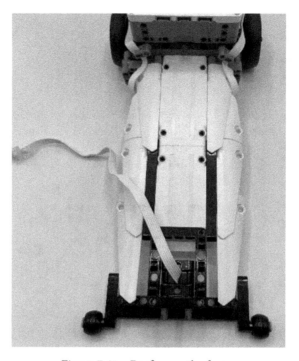

Figure 7.41 – Beefing up the frame

Next, find the following pieces:

- Two small white panel fairings
- One white *3L* beam
- Two blue connector pins

This is another quick and easy addition. Push the two blue connector pins through the two outside pinholes of the white beam. Connect the two white panel fairings to each side and connect this piece to the two blue pins at the front of the dragster:

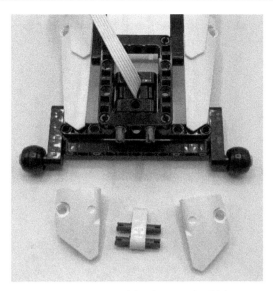

Figure 7.42 – Nose of the dragster build layout

Next, using two more white fairing pieces and four black connector pins, attach two more of the white fairing pieces right behind the parts you just added:

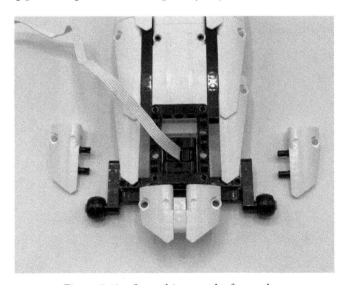

Figure 7.43 – Smoothing out the front edges

As you assemble these pieces to the dragster, you will start to see how the front of the dragster is taking shape and creating that aerodynamic look that you see in typical dragster body designs:

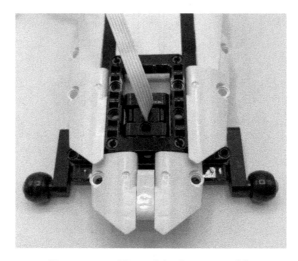

Figure 7.44 – View of the front assembly

Next, add four more black connector pins to the top of the open frame at the front of the dragster for the upcoming parts:

Figure 7.45 – Pins go on the open frame at the front of the dragster

You are closing in on the final details to the dragster. You will need the following pieces:

- Two white *11x3* curved panels
- One white *7x3* curved panel
- One black *11L* beam
- Two blue connector pins
- Four black connector pins
- One blue axle connector
- One wire clip

Begin with one of the *11x3* curved panels. Insert the blue connector pin with the *2L* sticking out. Slide on the black beam to these blue connector beams. Take your other *11x3* curved panel and add it to this piece but have its curve in the opposite direction. Using two black connector pins, attach the smaller *7x3* curved panel to the front. Lastly, add the wire clip to the side:

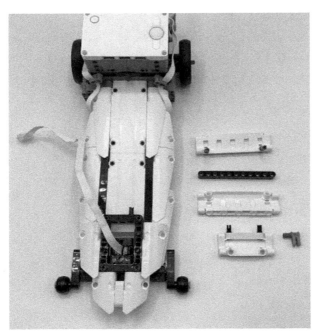

Figure 7.46 – Layout of the parts needed

Connect this piece using two black connector pins to the Intelligent Hub:

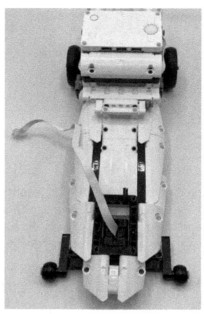

Figure 7.47 – This piece connects the Intelligent Hub to the body

You are at the final homestretch of the build. You will need the following parts:

- Two black *11L* beams
- One black *7L* beam
- Five teal *9L* beams
- Two white panel plates
- Two white small panel fairings
- One white *7x3* curved panel
- One white round spacer
- Eight black round elbows
- 16 blue axle connector pins
- One blue connector pin
- 18 black connector pins

Start with the white panel plate and flip it over on its backside. Using the blue axle connector pins and the black round elbows, connect one on each side and attach them to the white panel with a space between each one.

Add the black *7L* beam to the *7L* side of the white panel using two black connector pins. Next, connect the two small white fairing pieces together using a blue connector pin with one white spacer added to the *2L* side. Attach the two white panel fairing pieces to this blue connector pin. Clip this to the black *7L* beam using two black connector pins:

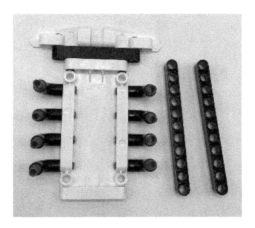

Figure 7.48 – Layout of the parts built for this piece

Grab the two black *11L* beams and connect all the black round elbow pieces to each beam, leaving two open holes on each side of the beam:

Figure 7.49 – Completed assembly

On the underside of each black beam, add three black connector pins: one pin on each end and one in the middle. Connect these black connector pins from both beams using the teal *9L* beam, securing this whole piece in place:

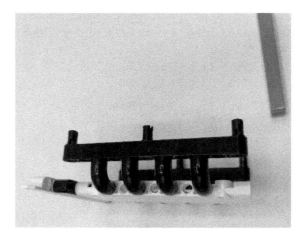

Figure 7.50 – Side view of the black connector pins

Using two black connector pins, add the second white panel plate to the end of the other white panel plate:

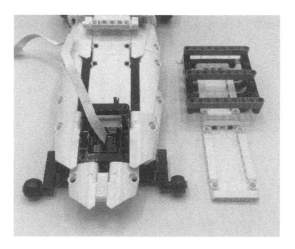

Figure 7.51 – The two build parts you should have at this point

Before we add this piece to the top of the dragster, slide the color sensor wire through the space between the white panel and teal beams. Add two more teal beams to the white panel. The teal beams will click onto the four black connector pins sitting atop the *5x7* open frame at the front of the dragster. The following figure has one black connector pin on the teal to showcase the black connector pins, which can be hard to see:

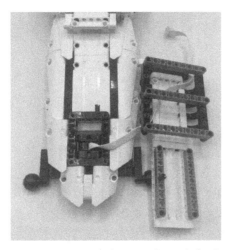

Figure 7.52 – Pass the wire through first!

Once everything is prepped, flip the part over and connect it to the top of the dragster. Ensure everything is properly connected and clipped into place:

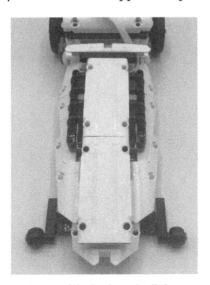

Figure 7.53 – View of the body with all things assembled

And now you have arrived at the last step. Take two black connector pins and the *7x3* curved panel plate and add them to the very front, giving the dragster the final look of a dragster racecar:

Figure 7.54 – Adding the nose of the dragster

This is how the completed dragster will look from the top:

Figure 7.55 – Top view of the completed dragster

And this is how it will look from the front:

Figure 7.56 – Front view of the completed dragster

You are now ready to add some code to bring this dragster to life. Let's rev our engines!

Programming the dragster

The code for this project is designed to achieve the following objectives:

- The dragster needs to count down *3-2-1* to make sure people have time to move out of the way.

- The dragster needs to stop when it sees the red finish line.

- The dragster needs to display the time to avoid human error when using a stopwatch.

The ports

Before we begin to code, you need to make sure you have all the parts properly connected to the Intelligent Hub. Start with the motors. The motors should be plugged into ports B and F. It does not matter which motor goes into which port as long as they are B and F. Both motors will simply move forward.

You will next connect your color sensor to the Intelligent Hub by clipping into part A. This sensor will help us stop at the finish line.

Dragster code program

In this section, you will walk through how to program the dragster to count down *3-2-1* and then take off at full throttle to achieve the fastest time on your track. You will code the color sensor to stop the motors as soon as the sensor detects the finish line color. Finally, you will write additional code to display your dragster race time so you can experiment to find the fastest design.

To begin, do the following:

1. Open up MINDSTORMS software.
2. Click on **Projects** at the bottom of the menu bar.
3. Scroll down to **Other** and click on **Create New Project**.
4. Choose to make a Words Blocks program.

Let's see the code next.

Main code section 1 sequence

The program has two main sections. You will build them step by step. Let's start with the first chunk of code:

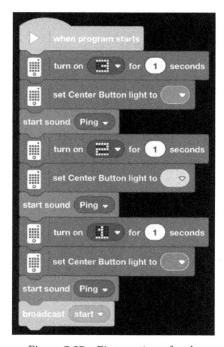

Figure 7.57 – First section of code

Let's see what these steps are:

1. Dragster matches begin with a countdown. You will add a 3-second countdown timer using the purple light blocks. We will display a number at each second counting down *3-2-1*. You can design your own numbers, shapes, or symbols. This gives time for the participant to back away from the track before the race begins.

2. In this coding example, a sound file named `Ping` (found in the audio library) has been added to give an audio countdown.

3. A color change is added, as well as using a purple light block that allows you to change the color of the center button. The color of the center light button changing from red to yellow to green mimics a stoplight or the dragster race light seen in many racetracks.

4. The final block of this section is a broadcast block found in the yellow **Events** section of the code. You will add this block and create a broadcast called **start**. This block is used to allow better flow of the code, as well as providing space to expand your code down the road when you experiment and tinker with new ideas.

Main code section 2 sequence

Now that the first section is done, ending with a broadcast signal of **start**, you need to write code for what happens when the signal is received:

1. Start with the **When I receive** broadcast block found in the yellow **Events** section of the code. Adjust this block to receive a **start** broadcast.

2. In the blue **Sensor** section, drag over a **reset timer** block. This will reset the internal timer to 0 to get an accurate reading of your dragster time on the course.

3. In the orange **Control** section, drag over a **Repeat Until** block. In this block, drag over a blue **Sensor** code block for when the color sensor sees a color. Adjust this to see red and make sure the sensor port is accurate.

4. Within this **Repeat Until** block, add two pink **Movement** blocks. The first will set the movement motors to **B** and **F**. The second will start the dragster moving to full power. Note the power is negative 100 as our gearing of only two gears inverts the direction in which the wheels spin.

5. Next, we have to write code for what happens once the color sensor sees red. As soon as the color sensor sees red, the repeat block kicks out of action and we continue down to our next coding block. In this case, we need the dragster to stop, using the pink **Movement** blocks to stop the motors. Drag over the **stop moving** block to do this.

6. Next, you want to see the time for how fast our dragster moved down the track. Create a variable in the orange **Variable** coding section named `time`. Drag over a **set variable** block and be sure the variable is `time` and in the blue **sensor** section of the coding panel. Drag over a **timer** block for the variable. This will grab the time as soon as the dragster crosses the finish line. If we don't do this, then the timer will continue to add time to the overall value.

7. Add an orange **Repeat** block from the **Control** section. In this example, the time will display three times so the designer has time to walk down the track and read the time being displayed.

8. Within the **Repeat** block, add a purple **Light** block that will write the `timer` variable on the *5x5* LED screen on the Intelligent Hub:

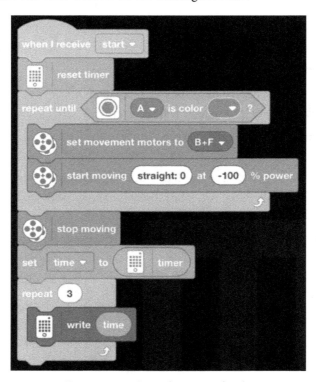

Figure 7.58 – Second section of code

In the end, the entire code will look like this:

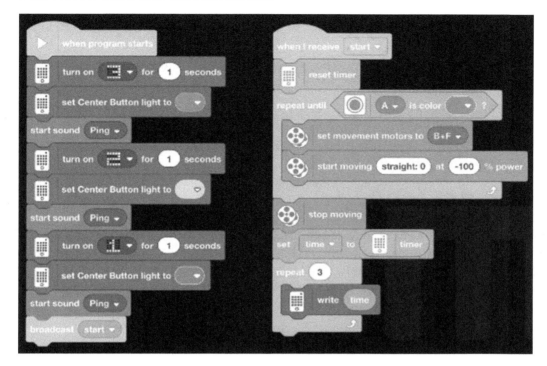

Figure 7.59 – Completed code

Go ahead and give it a try!

You have done it! You should have a working dragster that is full of potential and speed with plenty of room to modify and tweak to your design needs.

Create a test racetrack. Find a smooth surface to race your dragster. Use a tape measure and measure out a 10-foot track. Using tape, mark the starting line with one color (any color but red) and the finish line with red tape. If you do not have red tape, then use another color and adjust your code accordingly with the color sensor.

Enjoy!

Make it your own

And now it is time to hand the dragster over to you. This is where you can take what you have built so far and customize the dragster to your liking. Plenty of pieces have been left in the bin, such as designing aesthetic features, new approaches to making your dragster more intuitive, and plenty of coding options to take the dragster to the next level.

Here are a few ideas to consider:

- What can you change on the body of the dragster to look like a dragster you would drive?

- Search online for different dragster designs and tweak this model to another body design.

- If you don't want to use the color sensor, then how could you use the distance sensor to race down the track?

- What are other approaches to help your dragster become faster? Less weight, better gearing, and drag resistance reduction are a few things to consider.

Summary

In summary, we explored the concept of gearing up to increase the speed of your dragster. You also explored the timer block in the coding as well as the use of the broadcast block. Again, this is one of my favorite build challenges because you can spend hours designing the perfect dragster to become as fast as possible. It is a timeless activity that everyone loves.

In the next chapter, you will be building a decorator dragster that will allow you to design eggs and ornaments.

8
Building an Egg and Ornament Decorator

Around the holidays, we all love to design objects for the season. Having your kids or younger family members design objects such as ornaments and eggs can be a great way to pass some time, together as a family, and create some new traditions. In this chapter, you will be building a robot that will spin around objects such as eggs or ornaments for you to be able to design patterns using markers and other art materials. In the following image you can see how the build can be modified easily to decorate a round object like an ornament and also an egg:

Figure 8.1 – Top view of the decorator you will build in this chapter with both egg and ornament examples

In this chapter, we will break down the build and program as follows:

- Building the base frame
- Building the motor parts
- Adding motor parts to the base frame
- Adding the adjustable pieces to fit the size of the object
- Putting it all together
- Programming the robot to spin the object
- Decorating an egg and/or ornament

Technical requirements

To build the robot, all you will need is the Robot Inventor kit. For programming purposes, you will require the LEGO MINDSTORMS app/software.

Access to the code can be found here: `https://github.com/PacktPublishing/Smart-Robotics-with-LEGO-MINDSTORMS-Robot-Inventor/blob/main/Chapter%208%20Decorator%20Code.lms`.

If you would like a more detailed photo-by-photo build process of the robot, please head here to view the images: `https://bit.ly/30JTKCm`.

Building the robot

The strategy in the design of this decorator build is pretty straightforward. You require a design that can spin a round object to allow for your marker or pen to create smooth lines and designs. In order for this to happen, the robot build requires the following:

- It needs to be able to maintain a consistent speed of wheels.
- It needs to be adjustable to fit different sizes of objects.
- It needs to be smooth to keep objects from bouncing.
- It needs to be easy enough for any person or child to use.

By keeping these features in mind, you will understand why the frame and design is open, easily adjustable, and created in a way to quickly add and remove the object. While some additional building parts could have been added to make it more pleasing on the eye, following several test runs involving children, this version proved to be the easiest to use and manage.

Now that you understand the design goals, it is time to begin building the robot by starting with the base frame.

Building the base frame

To begin, you will create a very simple, yet sturdy, frame to house the decorator robot. For this, you will require the following parts:

- The Intelligent Hub
- One teal *11x19* base plate
- Two black *7x11* open frames
- Three teal *9L* beams
- Four blue connector pins
- Four black connector pins

Start by using the four blue connector pins and inserting the *2L* side through the *9L* beams and connecting them to the base plate. Insert the two blue connector pins into the second and sixth holes of two *9L* beams and attach both to the *11x19* base plate, as shown in the following photo:

Figure 8.2 – Teal base plate with teal beams added

Grab the two *7x11* open frames and connect them to the blue connector pins. Be sure that these open frames are lined up at the edge of the panel plate and the *9L* beams:

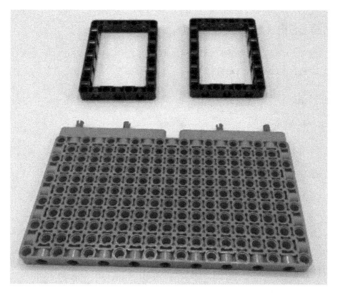

Figure 8.3 – Two 7x11 open frames

Secure the open frames in place using the third *9L* teal beam by using the two black connector pins to hold them in place:

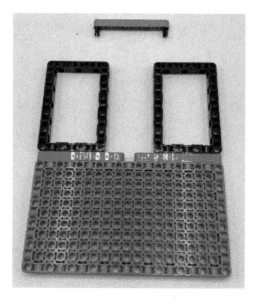

Figure 8.4 – 9L teal beam with black connector pins on the ends

The *9L* teal beam will hold the frames in place from the outside while they stay connected to the base plate on the other side:

Figure 8.5 – 9L teal beam for securing open frames to the base plate

The final step in this section involves using your final two black connector pins to secure the Intelligent Hub to the side of the panel plate. Slide the Intelligent Hub into place using the black pins to hold the Intelligent Hub in place next to the teal base plate:

Figure 8.6 – Base frame complete

The main base frame is complete. It is now time to add the motors to the build.

Building the motor parts

Let's move on to the motors. For this part, we will be doing a lot of copies of the same build, so be sure to take note of what you will be building twice.

You will require the following parts to begin the bases of the motor stands:

- Two black *5x7* open frames
- Four teal *3x3* Technic pieces
- One black *3L* beam
- Six black connector pins
- Six blue connector pins

Begin the setup by adding four black connector pins to one of the teal *3x3* pieces, two black connector pins to the second *3x3* teal piece, and then two blue connector pins to the third and fourth teal *3x3* pieces.

Then, add two blue connector pins to the outside holes of the *3L* black beam.

Check the placement of your connector pins with the help of the following photo:

Figure 8.7 – 3x3 teal pieces with pins

Once you have made sure you have properly connected the pins in the correct locations, go ahead and stack the *3x3* teal pieces. The teal *3x3* pieces with the blue connector pins will be on top. You will notice that one of these stacks has two black connector pins sticking out of the side. The other stack will add the black *3L* beam to the side:

Figure 8.8 – Teal pieces assembled

Once these are connected, slide them inside the open frames. One will have the black *3L* beam serving as a spacer, and the other will align right to the edge of the open frame:

Figure 8.9 – Teal pieces added to the open frame

Your next step involves adding the motors. Find the following pieces:

- Four motors
- Four yellow *5L* axles
- Four black *56x14* Technic wheels
- Four teal pin round connectors
- Two white axle connectors

For this build section, you will be making two sets of this part. You can build them at the same time to reduce time and page flipping.

Take the two motors and place them vertically on top of the teal *3x3* pieces using the blue connector pins sticking out of the top of the open frames:

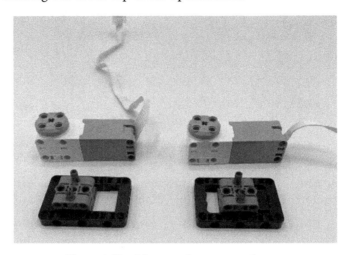

Figure 8.10 – Motors going on open frames

The motors will need to face each other:

Figure 8.11 – The motors should face one another

Insert the two yellow *5L* axle pieces in the middle of the motor:

Figure 8.12 – Yellow axle pieces added

Before you connect the motors together, you will need to slide in the two teal round connector pins:

Figure 8.13 – Round connectors for spacing

These are used for spacing only. They won't cause the axles to stick or anything like that. They are used to keep the wheels from moving out of position:

Figure 8.14 – Wheels are added next

Once you slide those onto the yellow axles, slide on the wheels and push them in so that they touch the teal round connector pins:

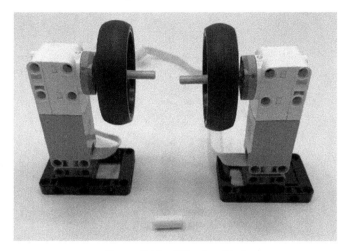

Figure 8.15 – Wheels added

The final step is to use the white *2L* axle connector to connect the two motors together:

Figure 8.16 – Motors connected

Once you have built them both, you will need to find a teal *9L* beam and two black connector pins to secure one set of motors together:

Figure 8.17 – Two motor sets

Here is a side view of the motor frames:

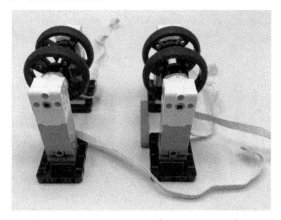

Figure 8.18 – Motor sets facing one another

Before you progress to the next part of the build, you should now have the following parts built and assembled:

Figure 8.19 – Assembled parts at this point in time

Now that you have checked to ensure that you have these parts all assembled, it is time to put them all together.

Adding the motor parts to the main frame

For this section, you will require the following parts:

- Four red connector pins with bush stops
- Four teal wire connectors

Take two of the red connector pins and the motor set that does not have the teal *9L* beam connecting the motors together that you just built:

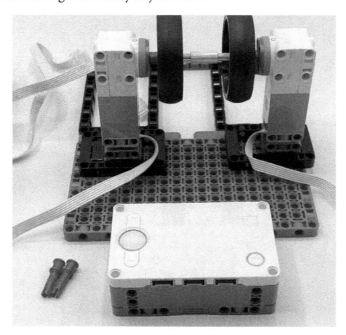

Figure 8.20 – Red pins required for connection

Place the motor part on top of the base plate and move it so that the back edge of the black open frames of the motor part are aligned with the fourth pin hole from the side of the base plate where the Intelligent Hub is connected:

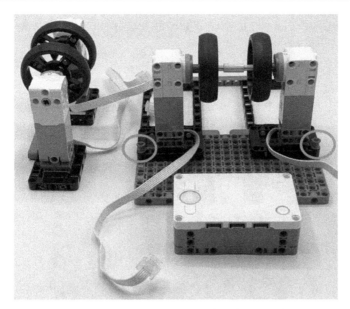

Figure 8.21 – Motor set one added to the main frame

Secure the motor part by adding the red connector pins to the corners:

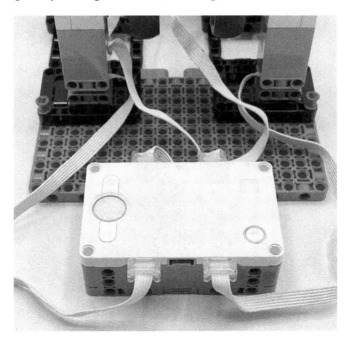

Figure 8.22 – Motor set one added to the main frame

Take the other motor part that has the teal *9L* beam connecting the motors and place it on top of the black open frames of the main base:

Figure 8.23 – Teal beams for support

For the sake of this build, we will connect the motors to the third pin hole of the open frame from the rear side:

Figure 8.24 – Teal beams added

This is also a good time to use the four teal wire connectors to make sure the wires are tucked away and low to the base to prevent them from impacting the wheels and motors.

Use them how you see fit, but you may want to begin by adding two the sides of the Intelligent Hub for one set of motors and the other connectors right in the middle of the base plate. Feel free to use more if required. The key is to keep them low and away from the motors:

Figure 8.25 – Wire clips for organizing the wires

Awesome! The main build of this robot is complete. It is now time to build some adjustable parts so that you can decorate various round objects.

Adding adjustable pieces to fit the size of object

You will require the following pieces for this next build section:

- One tan 20-tooth gear
- One black *12L* axle

You only need one of these, so this is quick and easy. Take the 20-tooth gear and simply slide it onto the end of the black *12L* axle. Set this aside as this part will be used when you actually decorate an ornament:

Figure 8.26 – Holder for ornaments

In this next part, you will be building two of the exact same parts to build a support frame for your round objects. The parts listed below are for two of these. You can either double the parts and build two at the same time, or build one and then come back and build another one later, whichever you prefer.

The parts required for both of these pieces are as follows:

- Two teal *9L* beams
- 16 black connector pins
- Four teal *3x5 L* beams
- Four black *3x5 L* beams
- Two black *15L* beams
- Two black *7L* beams
- Four teal *3L* beams
- 12 blue connector pins

To begin with, you will start with the teal *9L* beam:

Figure 8.27 – Teal 9L beam

Find two of the *3x5 L* beams and add two black connector pins to the bottom. Add each of these to the teal *9L* beam facing out and aligning with the edges:

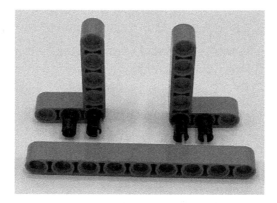

Figure 8.28 – 3x5 beams added to the beam

Take two of the blue connector pins and insert the *2L* side through the fourth hole on either edge of the *15L* black beam. Connect these blue connector pins to the teal part you just assembled:

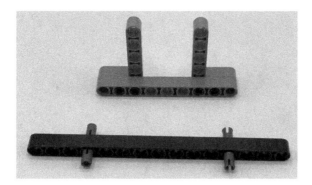

Figure 8.29 – Black beam with pins

Secure these teal pieces you just assembled to the black beam using the blue pins:

Figure 8.30 – Teal beams connected to the black beam

Using two more black connector pins, insert them at the top of the teal *3x5 L* beams:

Figure 8.31 – Black pins for the build

Attach the two black *3x5 L* beams facing outward. Secure these pieces in place by using two blue connector pins, inserting one underneath the black connector pin on each black *3x5 L* beam:

Figure 8.32 – 3x5 L beams added

Next, you will use the black *7L* beam:

Figure 8.33 – 7L beam to add support

Secure the build by connecting the beam across the black *3x5 L* beams using the blue connector pins available:

Figure 8.34 – 7L beam connected to the 3x5 L beams

Turn this piece around to the other side:

Figure 8.35 – Rear side of the build

Find your two teal *3L* beams. On both of these pieces, add a black connector pin to the outside hole and a blue connector pin to the middle hole. For the blue connector pin, insert the *1L* side of the pin connector to the teal *3L* beam, leaving the *2L* side exposed:

Figure 8.36 – 3L beam prep

Insert these pieces into the ends of the black *15L* beam:

Figure 8.37 – 3L beams added to the build

You will require two of these builds. If you have built two throughout this part, then please move on to the next part. Otherwise, head back to the top of this section and build another one of these parts.

You only have one teal Technic piece left in your kit. Locate this piece and two black connector pins. Add the two black connector pins to the sides of the pins in the middle of the teal *3x3* Technic piece:

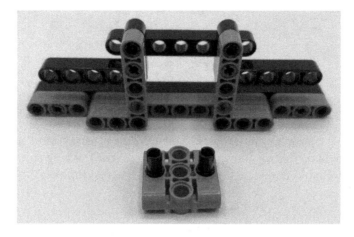

Figure 8.38 – 3x3 teal piece prep

Take one of the pieces you just built in the previous section and connect this piece in between the teal *3x5 L* beams. You only need to do this for one of these parts. This will help you keep the ornament steady when it spins, as you will see shortly:

Figure 8.39 – 3x3 teal piece added to the build

This is what your two parts that you have just completed should now look like:

Figure 8.40 – Two completed builds

Here is the side view:

Figure 8.41 – Side view of the builds

Here is the view from the top:

Figure 8.42 – Top view of the builds

Everything has now been built. Now, you just need to bring it all together, so let's do that and then move on to coding.

Putting it all together

OK. You are now in the final phase of this build. You should now have the following parts available if you followed all the preceding steps:

Figure 8.43 – Parts assembled at this point of the build

Based on the placement of the motor parts from earlier, you should now be able to attach the motor parts using the inside pins by connecting to the tops of the motors:

Figure 8.44 – Top parts added to the main frame

Using the 20-tooth gear and black axle part you assembled back in *Figure 8.26*, you can now insert the axle through any of the three vertical holes of the teal *3x5 L* beam. You will need to adjust which pin hole you use based on the round object you are trying to decorate. The axle piece is used for ornaments or any round object that has a hole for you to hold it in place. For an ornament, the hole in the ornament will be used to slide onto this axle piece. If you move the motor frames apart to the outside blue pins of the side pieces, that is roughly the size of a holiday ornament, and that is when you would use the axle to slide inside the ornament to hold it in place.

Currently, based on the steps performed in this chapter, you have the motors aligned and connected not to decorate an ornament, but to decorate an egg. When decorating an egg, you won't require the axle or gear element.

This is a side view of the decorator:

Figure 8.45 – Side view of the decorator

Here is a front view of the decorator:

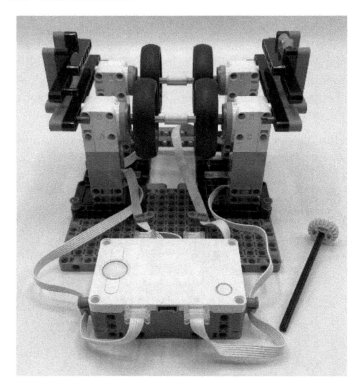

Figure 8.46 – Front view of the decorator

The key thing to remember regarding this build is that it is flexible and adjustable based on the round object you are trying to decorate. Now that you have a robot that can spin a round object and hold it in place, it is time to write the code to make it work.

Writing the code

Like all of our previous robots, when writing code, you need to think about the goals of the build and what needs to be accomplished. For this robot, there are three objectives to accomplish. The code you will write will achieve the following three objectives:

- Activation of all four motors to move at the same speed and smoothness
- Easy access to turn the program on and off using the Intelligent Hub power button
- Customization of the speed in the program to operate properly

It is time to make sure that everything is properly connected.

The ports

This robot does not use sensors. You are using all four motors, so let's be sure that all the motors are properly plugged into the proper ports. You have two sets of motors where two motors are connected together. One of these sets of motors need to be plugged into ports **F** and **B**. The second motor set needs to be plugged into ports **A** and **E**.

Once you have the motors properly plugged in and the wires secure and out of the way, it is time to write some code.

The decorator robot program

The program to activate the motors is relatively straightforward because you are essentially just turning the motors on and then turning them off. The key here to this program is to be sure that our motors are spinning in the same direction. The beauty of this project is that there is room to expand and tweak the code and build it to your liking:

1. Open up the **MINDSTORMS** software.

2. Click on **Projects** at the bottom of the menu bar.

3. Scroll down to **Other** and then click on **Create New Project**.

4. Choose to make a **Word Blocks** program.

5. Start with the **when program starts** block, which is the default block on the screen:

Figure 8.47 – First block of code for the program

6. The next three blocks you need will come from the pink **Movement** block section of your coding choices.

7. The first **movement** block will be the **set movement motors** block to identify which motors we are programming for. In this case, you will choose motor ports **F** and **B**.

8. The second **movement** block allows you to adjust the speed of the motors. Start with **70%**, but be aware that you can change the **%** figure to one of your choosing at any time.

9. The third **movement** block is the **start moving** block to activate the motors to start moving. You should have the following code if you have followed along correctly:

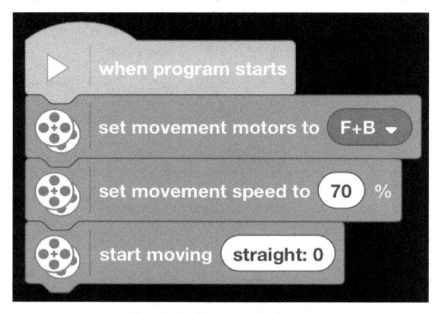

Figure 8.48 – Turning on the motors

10. Right-click the **when program starts** block if working on a computer, or press and hold if on a touchscreen, to activate the menu that will provide you with the option to **Duplicate**. Choose this option:

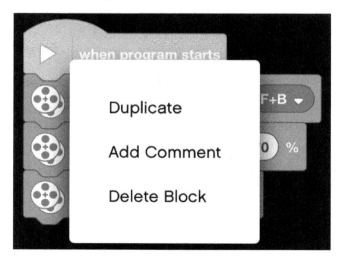

Figure 8.49 – Duplicate block option

11. You will keep everything the same except for two things. Change the motors to **A** and **E**. Also, change the movement speed to a negative 70% (-70):

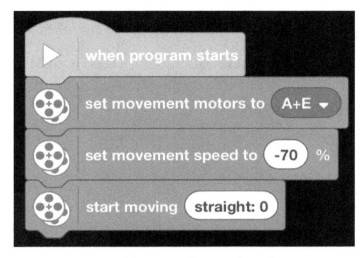

Figure 8.50 – Turning on the second set of motors

12. This is what your program should look like and it is now time to test out your build:

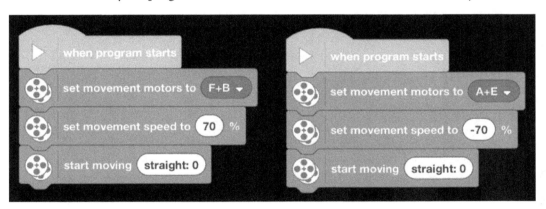

Figure 8.51 – Complete code view

This is the complete code you needed to write. Now that the decorator is complete, enjoy decorating! In order to decorate, you can sample various art supplies, such as markers, pencils, crayons, and paints, and so on. Try various techniques and patterns. Be sure to check out the demo video to see the robot in action. You will see that as the egg or ornament spins on the robot, you simply bring the tip of the marker (or other art material) to the edge of the object and, as the robot spins the object, you can now create various lines and patterns.

Maintenance tip

Depending on the types of markers and pens you use to design your egg or ornament, there is a good chance that some of the marker will bleed onto the wheels. As you experiment with colors and different objects, be sure to wipe down the wheels with a paper towel or wipe to prevent colors from ruining the egg or ornament. Additionally, you don't want your next robot build to leave marker stains on floors or tables either.

Making it your own

What can you do to make this build unique to your own needs? Here are some suggestions, and I look forward to your creative ideas.

Here are a few ideas to consider:

- How can you add new parts to allow lines to be added to an egg or ornament vertically?
- Could you add sensors to start/stop the program or perhaps increase/decrease the speed of the motors?
- What types of creative media can be used to decorate eggs and ornaments? Can you sample various art supplies, brushes, pencils, and markers? Can you add paper or foil and then decorate?
- Could you add a new piece that holds the pen/marker and decorate the object of your choice?

Summary

In summary, we explored the concept of rethinking what a robot can look like and what it can do. Oftentimes, we think of robots as being on wheels, resembling a vehicle or a humanoid. In this case, we took a classic activity that many people love to do and used a robotic build to spark new ideas with the robot, as well as design patterns on eggs and ornaments.

As you prepare to move on to *Chapter 9*, *Plankton*, where you will be building an interactive creature from a famous cartoon, you should be able to see how you can take the same parts and engineer all sorts of fascinating builds and designs using your imagination! Are you ready to take your building in a whole new direction? Let's do it!

9
Creating Plankton from SpongeBob SquarePants – Part 1

What better way to learn about robots than to create an iconic cartoon character? Of course, I am talking about Plankton from SpongeBob SquarePants. If only you had yellow and pink LEGO elements in the kit to build the whole cast! In this chapter, you will build a toy model of Plankton. This build is divided up into two chapters. This chapter focuses on building the main structure of Plankton. *Chapter 10, Creating Plankton from SpongeBob SquarePants - Part 2* focuses on the final touches to make him look more like Plankton and on interactive coding to bring the character to life. Let's dive into the sea of possibilities.

Here's what your Plankton model will look like by the end of these two chapters:

Figure 9.1 – The complete view of Plankton model you will build in this chapter

In this chapter, we will break down the build and program into the following sections:

- Building the robot
- Building the base of the frame
- Adding the motors for the arms
- Adding the color sensor
- Assembling the mouth
- Attaching the Intelligent Hub

Technical requirements

To build the robot, all you will need is the **Robot Inventor kit**. For programming, you will need the LEGO MINDSTORMS app/software.

Access to the code for this chapter can be found here:

`https://github.com/PacktPublishing/Smart-Robotics-with-LEGO-MINDSTORMS-Robot-Inventor/blob/main/Chapter%209%20Plankton%20Code.lms`

If you would like a more detailed photo-by-photo build process of the robot, please head here to view the images: `https://bit.ly/30IvZKK`.

Building the robot

The strategy in the design of Plankton is to consider the elements of the kit that will allow you to bring a cartoon character to life. In the end, you want to be able to interact with your build much like any animatronic toy. In order for this to happen, the robot build must have the following characteristics:

- Be able to turn its head from side to side
- Be able to move its arms
- Have animation of the eye to express emotion
- Be able to respond to the environment by using color and distance sensors
- Be able to speak popular phrases from the show

Keeping these features in mind, you will understand the building process. More importantly, you will be able to tweak this build to your liking by adding animations, phrases, and other responses to the environment as you see fit.

Building the base of the frame

You are going to start with the base of the robot body and prepare the first motor placement. In order to get started, you will need the following pieces from your kit:

- One teal *11x19* base plate
- One motor
- Three black *5x7* open frames

- Two red *3L* beams

- Four blue connector pins

- Ten black connector pins

To begin you will need following pieces from the preceding list:

Figure 9.2 – Parts layout

You will start by adding the four blue connector pins to the sides of the motor where the gear spins on the motor. Keep the *2L* side of the connector pin exposed.

This is illustrated in the following image:

Figure 9.3 – Connectors added to motor

Next, slide on the red *3L* beams on each side, as illustrated in the following image:

Figure 9.4 – Red 3L beams added to motor

Finally, clip on the black open frames on the *7L* side, making sure they are centered, as illustrated in the following image:

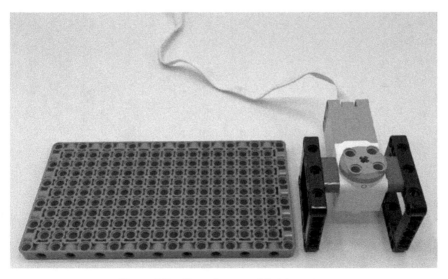

Figure 9.5 – Open frames added to motor

Now that you have that part built, go ahead and locate six black connector pins. These are shown in the following image:

Figure 9.6 – Six black connector pins

Invert the open frames so that they are on the ground, with the motor facing up. Add three black connector pins to each open frame on the opposite side of where you added the open frame to the motors, as illustrated in the following image:

Figure 9.7 – Black connector pins added to open frames

Go ahead and clip the motor and open frame to the teal base plate by centering the part in the middle of the plate and flush with one edge, as shown in the following image:

Figure 9.8 – Motor added to teal plate

Locate the third black *5x7* open frame and the final four black connector pins that you should have left. These are shown in the following image:

Figure 9.9 – Open frame and four black connector pins

Add a black connector pin to each of the four corners of the open frame, as illustrated in the following image:

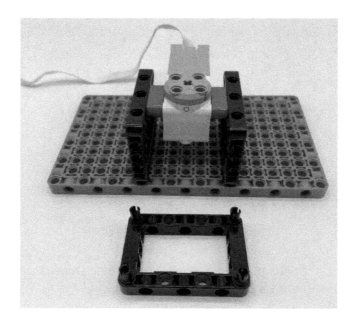

Figure 9.10 – Black connector pins added to open frame

Attach this open frame to the top of the other two open frames that are now attached to the teal *11x19* base plate, as illustrated in the following image:

Figure 9.11 – Open frame added to top of motor

This completes the frame for the motor that will allow the head to move back and forth. It's time to add two more motors for arm movement.

Adding the motors for the arms

Locate the following elements for the arms:

- Two motors
- Four black *3L* beams
- Six black connector pins
- Two gray connector perpendicular pins

The required pieces can be seen in the following image:

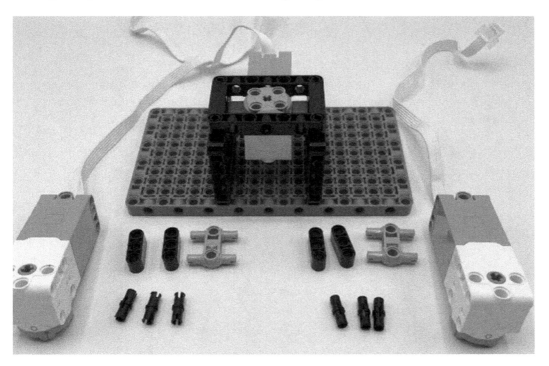

Figure 9.12 – Parts layout

Start this section by connecting the gray connector perpendicular pins to the gray part of the motors. It is easier if you have motors facing down, to ensure you properly build the part in the right direction to fit on the main frame. This is illustrated in the following image:

Figure 9.13 – Gray perpendicular pins added to motor

Next, add a black *3L* beam to the other end of the gray connector perpendicular pins and insert a black connector pin in the middle hole of the black *3L* beam, as illustrated in the following image:

Figure 9.14 – 3L beam added to motor

The next step is to locate the black *3L* beams that have not been used. Connect these black *3L* beams to the black *3L* beam already added to the motors in the previous step, as illustrated in the following image:

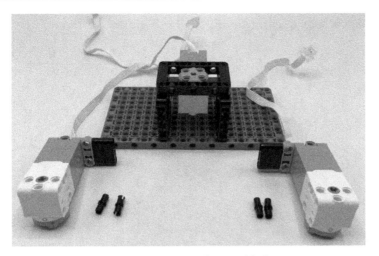

Figure 9.15 – Remaining 3L beam added to motor

Take your remaining black pins and add two to each of the motor parts on the outside holes of the black *3L* beam, as illustrated in the following image:

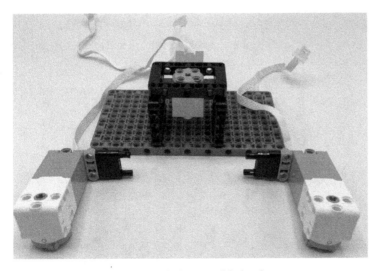

Figure 9.16 – Black pins added to beams

Once that is complete, go ahead and connect this to the teal *11x19* base plate, making each motor flush to the sides of the open frames. At this point, there is no structure under the part of the motor. Don't worry, as we will add that next. For now, just get everything properly lined up and put together.

Your build should now look like this:

Figure 9.17 – Motors added to main frame

Here is the view from the back, to make sure your motors are properly connected to the teal plate:

Figure 9.18 – Rear view of the main frame

Let's go ahead and get the other side of the motor supported. For this small support structure you will need the following pieces:

- Two gray perpendicular connector pins
- Two blue connector pins
- Four black *3L* beams

The required pieces can be seen in the following image:

Figure 9.19 – Parts layout

Insert one black *3L* beam to one side of a gray perpendicular connector pin. Do this to both gray pieces. Insert a blue connector pin, leaving the *2L* side exposed to the middle of the *3L* black beam you just added to the gray perpendicular piece. Slide the other black *3L* beam to this part.

The result can be seen in the following image:

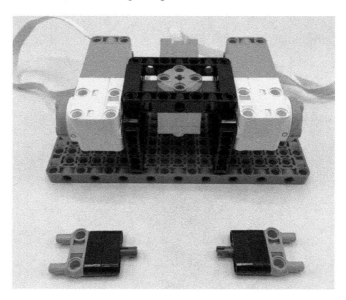

Figure 9.20 – Black beams added to gray perpendicular connector pins

Finally, connect the gray perpendicular connector pins to the motor and the remaining blue connector pin to the teal base plate.

At this point, here is how your build should look:

Figure 9.21 – Supports added to motors

You have now built the frame that will allow the head and arms to move. It's now time to add sensors for interaction.

Adding the color sensor

Let's begin to frame up the body a bit. In this section, you are going to build the front panel of Plankton that will house the color sensor, to give some interaction with the environment.

For this section, you will need the following pieces:

- Three teal *3x3* Technic pieces
- Seven blue connector pins
- Four teal *9L* beams
- One color sensor
- Twelve black connector pins

Before we add the front plate, you are going to add a couple of pieces to the top of the robot frame you have assembled so far while everything is exposed. Find one of the *3x3* teal Technic pieces and three blue connector pins. These pieces are illustrated in the following image:

Figure 9.22 – Parts layout

Add the *1L* side of the blue connector pins to the three holes of the top motor. Make sure before you do all of this that your motor is aligned to *0* as far as possible. Locate the gray dot and align it the best you can. Slide the teal *3x3* piece over the blue connector pins.

The result can be seen in the following image:

Figure 9.23 – Teal 3x3 piece added to middle motor

In the following screenshot, a layout has been put together to help you see how the front panel all comes together. This will form a front panel that clips to the open frames of the main frame using two black connector pins:

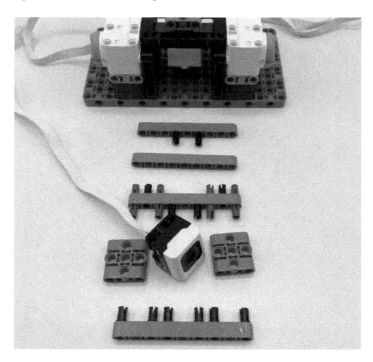

Figure 9.24 – Layout of sensor panel

Start with the teal *9L* beam that contains six black connector pins. Attach the teal *3x3* pieces to the sides of the beam and the color sensor in the middle. Everything should be flush at this point and should look like this:

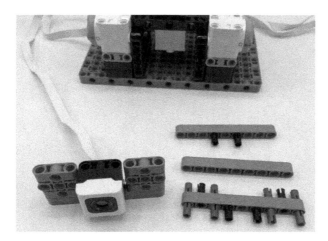

Figure 9.25 – Sensor and 3x3 pieces added to beam

Next, add the teal *9L* beam that contains four blue connector pins and four black connector pins to the top of the color sensor along with the *3x3* pieces. Be sure to use the side that connects to the color sensor (the side that has two black connector pins in the middle), as illustrated in the following image:

Figure 9.26 – Teal beam added to top of sensor

Connect the teal *9L* beam that is all by itself on top, as illustrated in the following image:

Figure 9.27 – Another teal beam added to the top

Follow this up by connecting the beam that has two black connector pins to the top of this build, as illustrated in the following image:

Figure 9.28 – Final teal beam added to the sensor panel

You now need to work to get this panel ready to be added to the front of the main frame. To do this, you will need the following parts:

- Two teal *3x5 L* pieces
- Two teal *2x4 L* pieces
- Ten black connector pins

Begin with the following pieces:

Figure 9.29 – Parts layout

Add four black connector pins to the top of the motors that are going to be used for the arms, as illustrated in the following image:

Figure 9.30 – Black connector pins added to motors

On these black connector pins, add the *3x5 L* pieces, as illustrated in the following image:

Figure 9.31 – 3x5 L beams added to connector pins

Flip the front panel with the color sensor to the back side. On the back side, insert a black connector pin in the middle of each of the *3x3* teal Technic pieces, as illustrated in the following image:

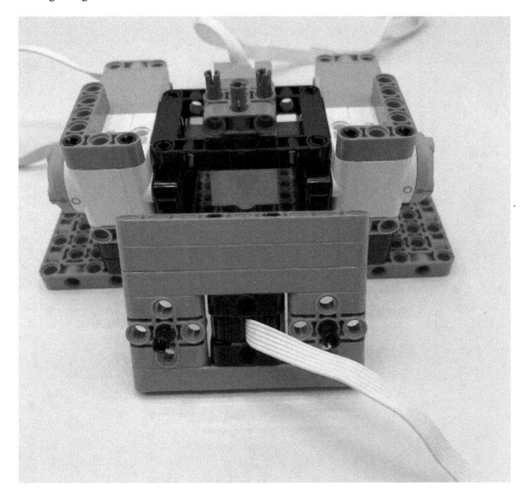

Figure 9.32 – Black connector pins added to sensor panel on back

Go ahead and clip this front panel to the front of the main frame where the top of the front panel is flush with the *L* beams you just added to the top of the motors, as illustrated in the following image:

Figure 9.33 – Sensor panel added to main frame

The last step in this section is to use your last four pieces from this collection. Use two black connector pins for each of the teal *2x4 L* pieces to strengthen the front panel to the main frame. Double-check that everything is properly secured and put together.

Your build should now look like this:

Figure 9.34 – 2x4 L beams added to top

The color sensor frame is now added to the base frame of the robot. The next part is the most exciting, because it begins to bring the build to life by creating a mouth that moves when speaking.

Assembling the mouth

For this next part of the build, it's important to pay attention to detail. Double-check your work and, as you go, test things out so that the mouth moves properly. There are several parts to this build, so this section will split the parts up as you go, to navigate through the parts easily.

To begin the mouth, you will need the following pieces:

- One motor
- Two teal *T* beams
- Four black connector pins
- One red axle connector pin
- One tan 12-tooth half-bevel gear

Begin by inserting the four black connector pins to the top two holes on the motor where the gear spins. Additionally, insert the red axle connector pin in the middle of the motor gear and slide the tan 12-tooth bevel gear onto the red axle connector pin, as illustrated in the following image:

Figure 9.35 – Four black connector pins, red axle, and gear added to motor

Next, take the two teal *T* beams and attach them to both sides of the motor with the middle beam of the *T* facing up, as illustrated in the following image:

Figure 9.36 – Teal T beams added to side of motor

You will now need to locate the following pieces:

- Six black connector pins
- Two gray axle bushings
- Two red *6L* axles
- One white axle connector
- Two teal *3x5 L* beams
- Two black 12-tooth double-bevel gears
- One tan 20-tooth double-bevel gear
- Two teal axle and pin perpendicular connectors

The required pieces can be seen in the following image:

Figure 9.37 – Parts layout

Start this part of the build by connecting the two red axles together using the white axle connector piece, as illustrated in the following image:

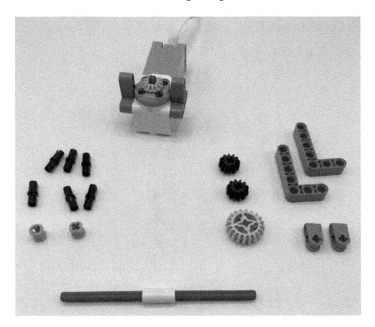

Figure 9.38 – Two red axles connected with white connector

Secondly, slide the tan 20-tooth double-bevel gear on the left-side red axle, as illustrated in the following image:

Figure 9.39 – Gear added to red axle

Next, add the gray bushings on both sides, whereby one is next to the tan gear and the other one is next to the white axle connector, as illustrated in the following image:

Figure 9.40 – Gray bushings added to red axles

Now, find your two *3x5 L* beams and insert two black connector pins into both on the *3L* side of the beam, as illustrated in the following image:

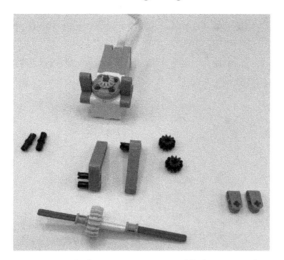

Figure 9.41 – Black connector pins added to 2x4 L beams

Using the *L* beams, attach them to the *T* pieces you added to the motor previously. A good way to do this is to first insert two black pins on the bottom pin holes of the *3L* side of the teal *3x5 L* beam. After you do this, then slide the teal *3x5 L* beam on the red axle through the top hole of the *3L* side of the *3x5 L* beam. Slide this part until it connects to the motor.

The result can be seen in the following image:

Figure 9.42 – 3x5 L beams added to motor

Important note

Please check that both the 20-tooth double-bevel gear and 12-tooth half-bevel gear are meshing with each other. A simple way to check is to simply move the motor manually, or write some simple code for turning on the motor.

Once your know your gears are meshing properly, then locate your two black 12-tooth gears and slide those onto both ends of the red axles, as illustrated in the following image:

Figure 9.43 – Black gears added to red axles

Follow this up by adding a teal axle and pin connector next to these gears. Finally, insert a black connector pin in the pin connector hole.

The result can be seen in the following image:

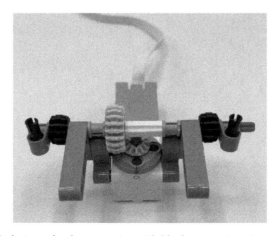

Figure 9.44 – Teal pin and axle connector with black connector pins added to red axle

Now, it's time to add the lips of the mouth. Find the following pieces:

- Four blue connector pins
- Six black connector pins
- Two teal *5L* beams
- One black *5L* beam
- One teal *9L* beam
- Two black *3x5 L* beams
- Two teal axle and pin perpendicular connectors with two holes

The required pieces can be seen in the following image:

Figure 9.45 – Parts layout

This section will start with the two black *L* beams. On the *3L* side of each beam, add two black connector pins. On the other end of the *5L* side of the *L* piece, add two blue connector pins using the *2L* side of the connector pin.

The result can be seen in the following image:

Figure 9.46 – 3x5 L beams with connector pins added

Beneath these *L* pieces, connect the teal *5L* beams to each one, followed by the teal *9L* beam, joining the two black *L* beams together into one piece, as illustrated in the following image:

Figure 9.47 – 3x5 L beams attached to the teal 9L beam

Next, add the black *5L* beam to the top of the teal *9L* beam, using the final two black connector pins, as illustrated in the following image:

Figure 9.48 – Black 5L beam attached

To complete this part of the build, connect the teal axle and pin connector pieces to the blue connector pins exposed on both ends, as illustrated in the following image:

Figure 9.49 – Teal pin and axle connectors added to ends

Now, we need to add this mouth part to the motor frame, using gears and axles. Find the following parts to be able to do this:

- Two brown *3L* axles with stops at one end
- Two tan 20-tooth double-bevel gears

The required pieces can be seen in the following image:

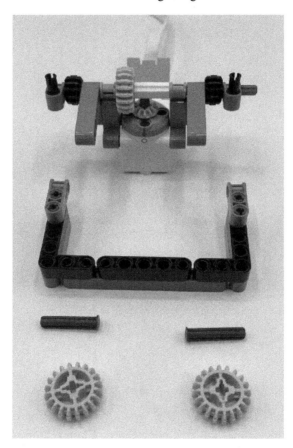

Figure 9.50 – Parts layout

Insert the brown axles through the inner side of both teal *3x5 L* beams that are currently attached to your motor frame. See the following images for proper hole alignment, but double-check that you have added the brown axle piece into the third pin hole from the end of the *L* piece:

Figure 9.51 – Gears added to motor

Once you have the brown axles inserted properly, then add the tan 20-tooth gears on both sides, as illustrated in the following image:

Figure 9.52 – Side view of the gears and placement of parts

Next, all you have to do is add the mouth part to the brown axle part that is sticking out on either side. Double-check that your brown axles are properly lined up so that this part is straight. It is easy to connect this mouth part and later realize that the mouth is crooked and moving at a slant. Take time to adjust it. You might have to keep adjusting as you keep building it, which is okay, but start now with proper alignment.

The result should look like this:

Figure 9.53 – Front view of bottom jaw

This next part is a quick build and is one we will come back to later. These are the supports that will eventually help with the head portion of the build. You need to add this now, or otherwise it will be too difficult to add later.

You will need the following pieces:

- Two teal 9L beams
- Two black connector pins

The required pieces can be seen in the following image:

Figure 9.54 – Parts layout

Using the black connector pins, connect the *9L* beams to the end of the *L* beams attached to the main frame. They won't stay perfectly upright at this point and that is okay—you will come back to these pieces later.

The result should look like this:

Figure 9.55 – Teal beams added to mouth

We have one part of the mouth complete, but it is hard to talk with only half a mouth. You need to find these pieces to build the next part of the mouth:

- Two black *7L* beams

- One teal *9L* beam

- Two teal *3x5 L* beams

- Nine black connector pins

- One black round connector

The required pieces can be seen in the following image:

Figure 9.56 – Parts layout for upper mouth

You can see the general layout of this build in the previous image, but to start, go ahead and add the black connector pins to the black *L* pieces. Each piece will have four of the black connector pins inserted. The ninth black connector pin will go in the black round connector piece, as shown in the following image:

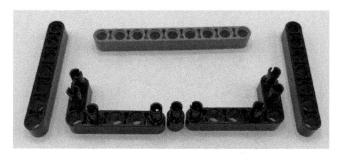

Figure 9.57 – Black connector pins added to 3x5 L beams

Next, use the teal *9L* beam and connect the two *L* beams and the black round connector. If done right, there will be one hole left on each end. Add the two black *7L* beams to the top of the *L* beams. In the end, you should have another part that looks like the second half of the mouth, as illustrated in the following image:

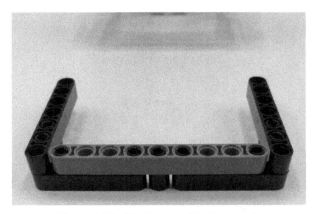

Figure 9.58 – Teal beam added to mouth

Add this piece to the main frame of the robot build. There should be a pin to connect this piece to the top of the other mouth part you added previously. Check the next three images to see different angles, to ensure you have this part connected properly. This first image shows the upper mouth:

Figure 9.59 – Upper mouth added to mouth build

It is important that at this point you check the axles for these parts, to make sure the teal axle and pin perpendicular connectors are aligned to not collide and allow the mouth to open and close. You might need to adjust the axles to get them dialed in properly.

A side view of the mouth can be seen here:

Figure 9.60 – Side view of the mouth

Note how one side will have about *1L* of the red axle exposed, while the other side will not. This is how it is supposed to be. Remember that you added the tan bevel gear to one side of the red axle, which puts things off slightly. You will cover this red piece at the end, so there's no need to worry.

Here, you can see a rear view of the mouth:

Figure 9.61 – Rear view of the mouth

Now that you have a mouth built and designed, it's time to add the Intelligent Hub so that you can begin to form the face and also allow for coding to happen.

Attaching the Intelligent Hub

This next part is the really exciting part because this is where you will add the brains of the operation—you will start to see Plankton come to life with this section of building.

To kick things off, you will need the following pieces:

- Two black *5x7* open frames
- Eight black connector pins

The required pieces can be seen in the following image:

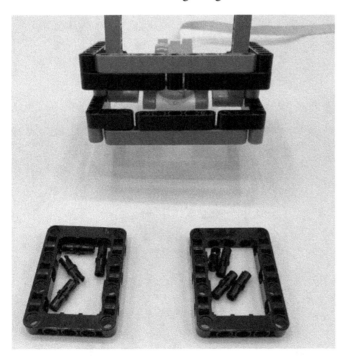

Figure 9.62 – Parts layout

Each open frame will have four black connector pins attached to it. Two will be on the edge pin holes, on the *5L* side. Along the *7L* side at the bottom, add the other two black connector pins, as illustrated in the following image:

Figure 9.63 – Black connector pins added to open frames

Using these two black connector pins, connect each open frame to the motor that will activate the mouth of the robot, as illustrated in the following image:

Figure 9.64 – Open frames added to mouth motor

Here is a back view so that you are able to see how these frames look from the back side:

Figure 9.65 – Back view of open frames added to mouth motor

You will now add some support beams to hold the Intelligent Hub up. Locate the following parts:

- Two black double-bent Technic beams
- Two black *5L* beams
- Two black connector pins
- Two blue axle pin connectors

The required pieces can be seen in the following image:

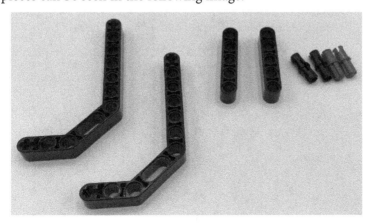

Figure 9.66 – Parts layout to hold up Intelligent Hub

Start with the two black *5L* beams. Attach these to both open frames, using the black connector pins that are available on the open frames.

The result should look like this:

Figure 9.67 – 5L beams added to open frames

On the second and third pin holes of the *5L* beam closest to the gears, add a black connector pin and a blue connector pin, respectively, as illustrated in the following image:

Figure 9.68 – Connector pins added to 5L beams

Attach the bent Technic beams to these two pins, as illustrated in the following image:

Figure 9.69 – Double bent beams added to the connector pins

Now that the support brackets are in place, it's time to add the Intelligent Hub. Locate the following pieces:

- One Intelligent Hub
- One black *7x11* open frame
- Two teal *T* beams
- Two blue connector pins
- Eight black connector pins

The required pieces can be seen in the following image:

Figure 9.70 – Parts layout of Intelligent Hub frame

Begin this portion of the build by adding a blue connector pin and a black connector pin on both sides of the Intelligent Hub, on the side of the hub that has the main power button, as illustrated in the following image:

Figure 9.71 – Connector pins added to side of Intelligent Hub

Once these are inserted, slide a teal *T* beam onto both sides using those connector pins, as illustrated in the following image:

Figure 9.72 – T beams added to sides of Intelligent Hub

Using four more black connector pins, add one to each corner of the face of the Intelligent Hub. Use two more black connector pins to add to the sides of the *7x11* open frame, as illustrated in the following image:

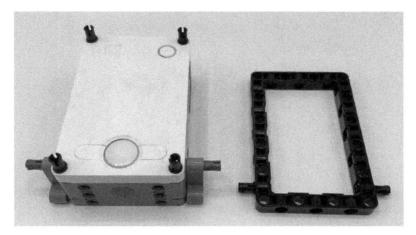

Figure 9.73 – Black connector pins added to front of Intelligent Hub

Attach the open frame to the top of the Intelligent Hub, as illustrated in the following image:

Figure 9.74 – Open frame added to top of Intelligent Hub

You will now need the following builds that you have assembled so far:

Figure 9.75 – Two parts built up until this point for the mouth and face

You now have these two build parts assembled, and it's time to join them together. To do this, you need to attach the Intelligent Hub to the teal *9L* beams you added to the motor frame previously. Make sure the teal *9L* beam connects to the black connector pin of the *7x11* open frame that is on the Intelligent Hub.

The result should look like this:

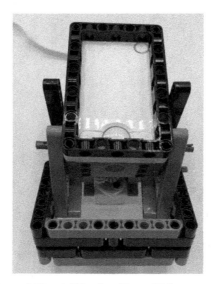

Figure 9.76 – Adding Intelligent Hub to mouth

Here is a closer view of how it all attaches:

Figure 9.77 – Closer view of how Intelligent Hub attaches to mouth

Find the following parts:

- Four black connector pins
- Two black axle and double pin connectors

The required pieces can be seen in the following image:

Figure 9.78 – Parts layout to secure Intelligent Hub

This part can be a bit tricky so take your time, and if you need to grab another set of hands to help you out, then please do so.

Here is a side view of where the parts will go:

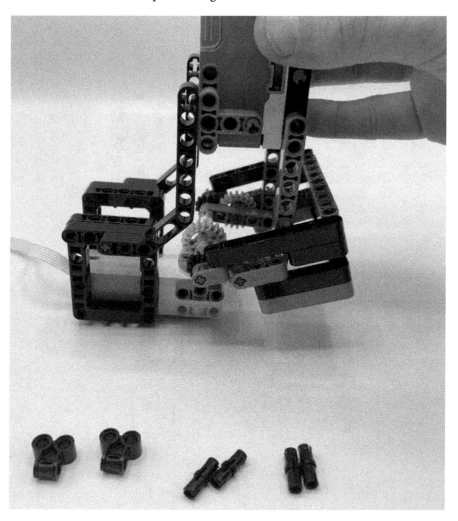

Figure 9.79 – Side view of where the parts will go

Start by lining up the Intelligent Hub to the black double-bent support beams that have already been added in the previous step (see *Figure 9.69*), as illustrated in the following image:

Figure 9.80 – Placement of parts to hold Intelligent Hub upright

Using the black axle and double pin connectors on both sides and the black connector pins, connect the black bent beams and the Intelligent Hub using these parts.

The result should look like this:

Figure 9.81 – Front view of face and mouth

Let's finally join all the parts together. You should now have the following two parts:

Figure 9.82 – Head and main frame builds

The motor of the head part will connect to the three blue connector pins on the motor of the base frame, as illustrated in the following image:

Figure 9.83 – Face and mouth added to main frame

The robot is coming together—its general frame and outline are now complete. The mouth, arm motors, neck motor, and Intelligent Hub are properly placed. It's now time to add additional parts to make the robot look like Plankton.

Summary

In summary, you designed the first part of Plankton. You explored some new ways of using gears to build a mouth that moves, along with inserting sensors. Additionally, you have positioned the Intelligent Hub to serve as a face. Using many of these techniques, your Plankton is almost ready for animatronic action.

In the next chapter, you will continue this build by adding all the aesthetic details and writing some code to bring the robot to life.

10
Creating Plankton from SpongeBob SquarePants – Part 2

In the previous chapter, you built Plankton's frame. The major components, frame, and sensor have all been installed. What comes next is adding additional elements to make the robot look more like Plankton and write code to bring it to life.

In this chapter, we will continue to develop the robot by doing the following:

- Adding final details to give the appearance of Plankton
- Programming the robot to be interactive

Technical requirements

To build the robot, all you will need is the Robot Inventor kit. For programming, you will require the LEGO MINDSTORMS app/software.

Access to the code can be found here: https://github.com/PacktPublishing/Smart-Robotics-with-LEGO-MINDSTORMS-Robot-Inventor/blob/main/Chapter%209%20Plankton%20Code.lms.

If you would like a more detailed photo-by-photo build process of the robot, please refer to the following link to view the images: `https://bit.ly/3cDrHdw`.

Adding the aesthetic details

Alright, you are closing in on this build. It is time to add the details that will make the robot feel more like a robotic Plankton!

Let's get started by locating the following pieces:

- Eight blue connector pins
- Six black connector pins
- Four teal *5L* beams
- Four teal *3L* beams
- Two teal *3x5 L* beams
- Two teal *2x4 L* beams

Here is a visual of the parts needed for this section:

Figure 10.1 – Laying out parts to bring Plankton to life

Start with the main build and turn to the side of the Intelligent Hub. Add one black connector pin and one *3x5 L* beam to each side of the Intelligent Hub:

Figure 10.2 – 3x5 L beams added to the side of the Intelligent Hub

Next, add four blue connector pins along the black open frame attached to the front of the Intelligent Hub, leaving the *2L* side of the pin exposed:

Figure 10.3 – Blue axle pins added to the open frame

Add a teal *3L* beam and a *5L* beam to the blue connector pins to begin to build out the teal cover for Plankton:

Figure 10.4 – 3L and 5L beams added to the open frame

Add a black connector pin right below the last blue connector pin that is exposed. Note the following image where the finger is showcasing where to insert the pin:

Figure 10.5 – Black pin added below the blue axle pin

Add a teal *2x4 L* beam to the bottom and then a teal *5L* beam covering the pin connectors:

Figure 10.6 – 2x4 L beam and a 5L beam added to the side

Once you have done that, insert another black connector pin in the top corner. Lastly, cover that up with a teal *3L* beam:

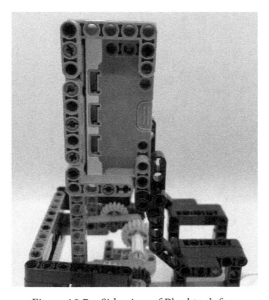

Figure 10.7 – Side view of Plankton's face

Here is how it should appear when complete:

Figure 10.8 – Front side view of Plankton's face

Here is the front facing view where you can start to see the robot taking shape. The Intelligent Hub will serve as the face once you get to the programming phase:

Figure 10.9 – Front view of Plankton

For the next layer of detail, locate the following parts:

- Six black connector pins
- One black *7L* beam
- Two teal *3x3* Technic pieces

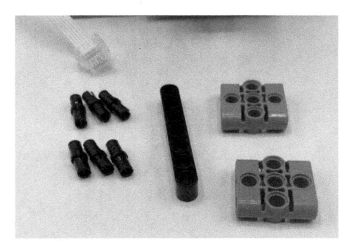

Figure 10.10 – Layout of parts for the face

Add a black connector pin to both ends of the black *7L* beam. Connect the beam to the two *3x3* teal pieces. They will be moveable at this point because of the single pin connecting them to the black beam, but that is OK. Insert a black connector pin in the middle hole of each of the *3x3* Technic pieces:

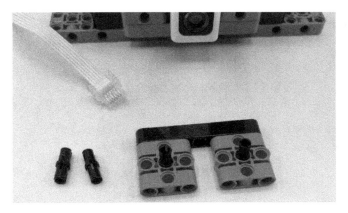

Figure 10.11 – 3x3 teal pieces connected with a black 7L beam

Using the final two black connector pins, you will add these to the main frame of the build. Locate the pin holes that are directly underneath the Intelligent Hub and insert them as shown in the following image:

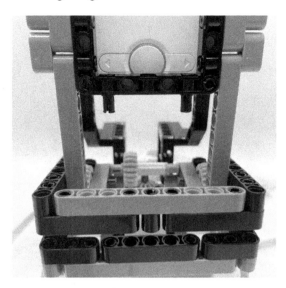

Figure 10.12 – Black pins added under the Intelligent Hub

Insert the piece into the black connector pins. You may have to be patient to get a good hold, but it should work out just fine:

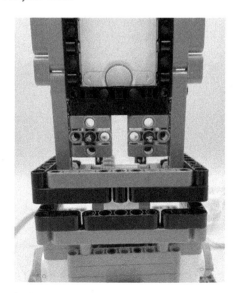

Figure 10.13 – Black beam with two 3x3 teal pieces added to the black pins

Locate the following pieces next:

- Ten black connector pins
- Three teal *9L* beams
- Three teal *3x3* Technic pieces

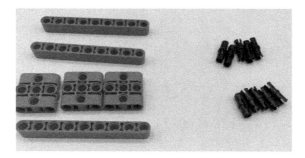

Figure 10.14 – Layout of parts for Plankton's face

Start this part by adding two black connector pins to the bottom of each of the three teal *3x3* Technic pieces:

Figure 10.15 – Preparation for the 3x3 teal pieces

Next, attach one of the teal *9L* beams to these three pieces:

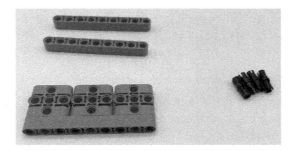

Figure 10.16 – 3x3 pieces connected on the 9L beam

Then, add two black connector pins to the outside teal *3x3* pieces:

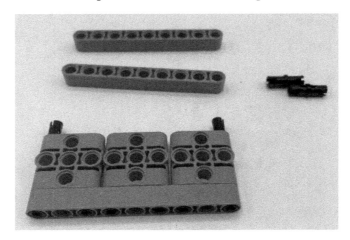

Figure 10.17 – Black pins added to the outside of the 3x3 elements

Next, add a teal *9L* beam to the top, followed up by two more black connector pins to add the final teal *9L* beam:

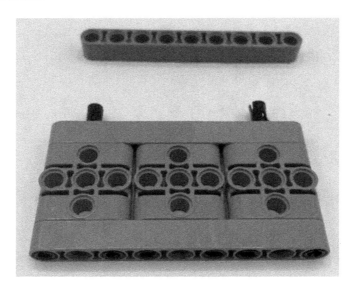

Figure 10.18 – 9L beam added to the top of the 3x3 elements

This part will clip onto the main frame where you just added the part right below Intelligent Hub. Use the two black connector pins sticking out of the center pin hole to secure this piece to the main frame.

Here is how it should appear at this point:

Figure 10.19 – Add this build piece to the underside of Plankton's face and above the mouth

You are getting super close to the end! There are just a few more final details to enhance this robot build. Locate the following pieces:

- Six black connector pins
- Two teal *2x4 L* beams
- Two teal *5L* beams

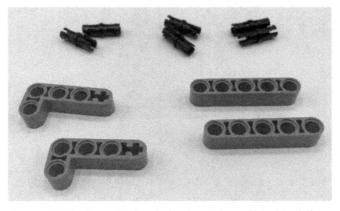

Figure 10.20 – Layout of parts for the outline of Plankton's face

Start by adding the black connector pins around the open frame that is attached to the front of the Intelligent Hub:

Figure 10.21 – Black pins added to the open frame

Add the teal *2x4 L* beams to the bottom corners facing out, along with the *5L* beams on top of the *L* beams. This will leave the top exposed, as demonstrated in the following image:

Figure 10.22 – Teal 2x4 L beams and 5L beams added to the open frame

You are going to add Plankton's eyebrow next. To do this, you will require the following parts:

- One yellow *5L* axle
- One teal *9L* beam
- One black *1L* round connector
- One black *2L* round connector
- Two black elbow connector pins
- Two black connector pins
- Two blue connector pins

Figure 10.23 – Layout of parts for the eyebrow

First, take the yellow axle piece and slide one of the black *2L* and *1L* round connectors to the middle. Secure them in place using the curved connectors on either side. Then, insert a blue connector pin at the ends of each curved connector:

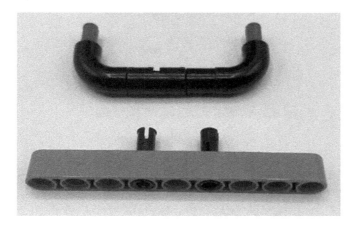

Figure 10.24 – 7L beam and eyebrow build

Then, on the teal beam, add a black connector pin on the fourth pin hole from the edge on both sides:

Figure 10.25 – Eyebrow build complete

Next, add the eyebrow piece to the opposite side of the teal beam that has two black connector pins sticking out.

Add this piece to the top of the head of Plankton:

Figure 10.26 – Eyebrow added to Plankton's face

The face is now complete, so it is time to build out the arms to add to the arm motors.

Building the arms

This is the final build part for the robot before you get to code and bring your Plankton to life! You are going to build two simple arms to bring some extra character and movement to your robot.

To do this, you will require the following parts:

- 12 black connector pins
- Two teal *9L* beams
- Two teal *T* beams
- Four teal *3L* beams
- Four round teal connectors
- Two blue connector pins

Figure 10.27 – Layout of parts for the arms

Insert the blue connector pins to the ends of both *9L* beams. Cover up the blue connector pins with the round teal connector pieces:

Figure 10.28 – Round connectors added to the 9L beams

Insert two black connector pins to all of the *3L* beams and *T* beams:

Figure 10.29 – Black pins added to the parts

From here, go ahead and connect these parts to the *9L* beams to complete the arms:

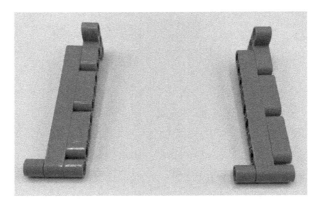

Figure 10.30 – Arms assembled

Using your final four black connector pins, add two to each of the *T* pieces to connect the arms to the motors:

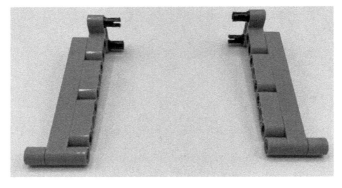

Figure 10.31 – Black pins added

And finally, you add the antenna. Find the two antenna pieces and two gray connector pins:

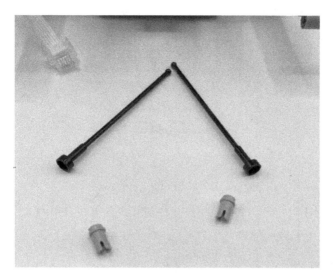

Figure 10.32 – Antenna parts

Insert the pins in the top of the head and attach the antenna:

Figure 10.33 – Arms and antenna added to Plankton

And now for the final part! Find the round teal element:

Figure 10.34 – Round connector

Use this round teal part to hide the small red axle part exposed on the side:

Figure 10.35 – Round connector added to the red axle

And with that you have successfully built Plankton! Let's now bring him to life, complete with all his crankiness!

Figure 10.36 – Complete build of Plankton

This is a good time to work to hide the wires behind Plankton using wire clips. Ensure that they are not so tight that the wires can't move as Plankton moves:

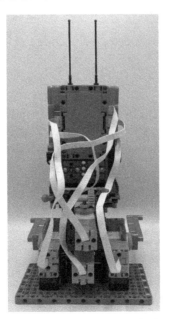

Figure 10.37 – Back view of Plankton

Double-check your build from this side, along with the front and back views of the previous images:

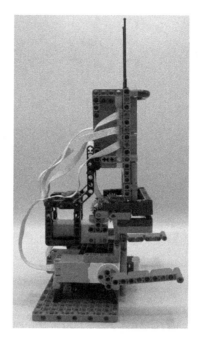

Figure 10.38 – Side view of Plankton

The build is now complete. It is now time to write code to bring the robot to life.

Writing the code

You have this wonderful Plankton build and it is only cool if it indeed moves and interacts with the environment. This code will walk you through some ways to bring Plankton to life, while providing enough openness to be tweaked to your liking.

The code for this project is designed to achieve the following objectives:

- Use two motors to create arm movement.
- Use one motor to enable the head to turn.
- Use one motor to open and close the mouth.
- Use a color sensor to code voice or movements.
- Use a distance sensor to trigger responses.

The ports

Before you dive into the code, let's be sure that your motors and sensors are properly plugged into the proper ports. The neck motor, which will allow Plankton to move to the left and right, should be in port **A**. The motor that opens and closes the mouth needs to be in port **C**. The arms will be in ports **D** and **E**. The color sensor on the front of Plankton will be plugged into port **F**. Later, if you want to add the distance sensor for some optional coding and interactions, then that will go into port **B**.

Plankton robot program

Again, this code will get your build up and running while providing you with lots of room for your own unique style to be infused as you wish. Just take things one step at a time and you should be up and running in no time.

When the program starts the code

This section of code will be the code for what happens when the robot starts up. It is basically designed to calibrate the robot to the same original position before engaging in interactions:

1. Open up the **MINDSTORMS** software.
2. Click on **Projects** at the bottom of the menu bar.
3. Scroll down to **Other** and click on **Create New Project**.
4. Choose to make a **Words Blocks** program
5. Start with the **When Program Starts** block, which is the default block on the screen:

Figure 10.39 – The start block to begin coding

6. Create a **Variable** named Voices in the **Orange Variable** section:

*   Select **Make a Variable**.
*   Name it Voices.

7. Drag the **Set Variable To** block under the **when program starts** block.
8. Insert a purple **Light** block called **turn on** and design the eye of Plankton.

9. Insert a purple **Light** block called **set Center Button light to** and change it to **black** so it is off when in use.

10. Insert two blue **Motor** blocks called **set speed to**. Change the speed to **10%**. One blue motor block will be for motor **A**, and the second block for motor **C**.

11. Insert four blue **Motor** blocks called **go to shortest path** to position **0**. Make one block for motors **A**, **C**, **D**, and **E**. This will reset the robot to its original position before anything begins.

12. Insert two yellow **Events** blocks called **broadcast**. Name one Mouth and the other Neck. This will eventually activate movements for the mouth and neck.

13. Insert an orange **Control** block called **wait** and make this .5 seconds.

14. Insert a purple **Sound** block called **start sound**. From this menu, you can choose a sound from the library or, if you have any Plankton sound files of your own, you can add these here.

15. Insert an orange **Control** block called **repeat**. Make the repeat block repeat for *three* cycles. Inside the **repeat** block, add a purple **Light** block called **start animation**. When you click on the drop-down menu, you will see the following options:

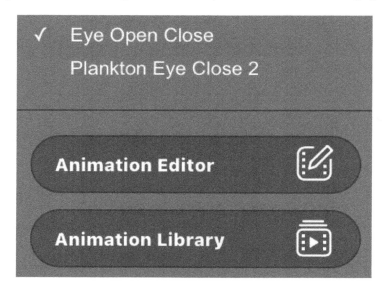

Figure 10.40 – Menu to create your own animation

16. Choose **Animation Editor**.

17. Design your own animation of the eyes opening and closing, or you can use the one I made, which is found in the coding example:

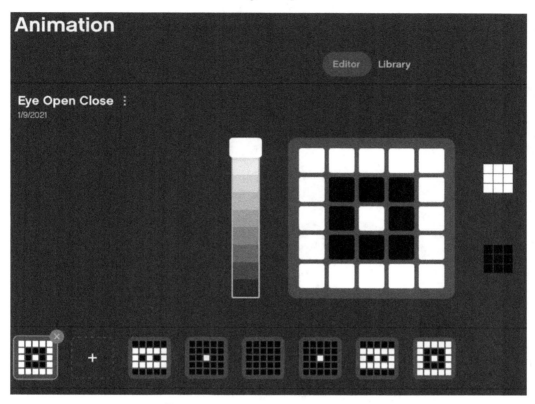

Figure 10.41 – Animation creation panel

18. Be sure to select the animation from the drop-down menu that you created.

19. Insert an orange **Control** block named **wait** under the **Animation** block. Start at . 25, but you can adjust this to your liking so that the animations are viewable.

Here is what this code should look like when complete:

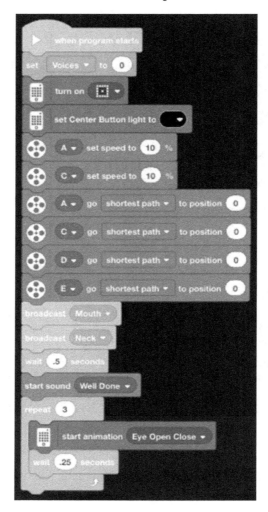

Figure 10.42 – Complete view of the program when it starts

Now that you have the robot calibrated, it is time to write some code to interact with its environment. Let's now take a look at some options for the color sensor.

Color sensor code

This section will walk you through the code for the color sensor. You can adjust the colors as well as what you want to have happen when a color is detected. For this example, you will program for sound effects. You will code one of these sections and then duplicate as many times as you wish for other colors:

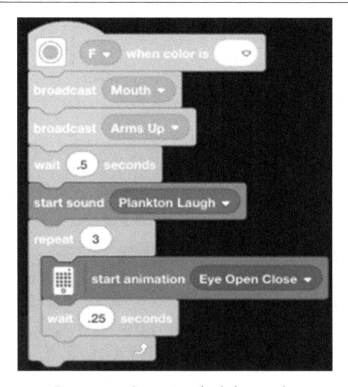

Figure 10.43 – One section of code for one color

1. Insert a yellow **Events** block for **when color is** and choose a color. In this example, white is used.

2. Insert two yellow **Events** blocks named **broadcast** and make one say Mouth and the other Arms Up.

3. Insert an orange **Control** block named **wait** and set that block to .5 seconds.

4. Insert a purple **Sound** block named **start sound** and select the sound file of your choice.

5. Insert an orange **Control** block named **repeat** and set that to 3. Inside the **repeat** block, add a purple **Light** block called **start animation** and choose the same animation you designed previously, or create a new one if you prefer.

6. Insert an orange **Control** block named **wait** and set that block to .5 seconds.

Repeat this process for other colors by right-clicking on this section of code and choosing **Duplicate**:

Duplicate

Add Comment

Delete Block

Figure 10.44 – Duplicate option to copy code

Here is what the code looks like at the end for the demo code; four colors with four different phrases. Note that one of these has different animations and movements, so remember you can tweak each one to your liking to do different things:

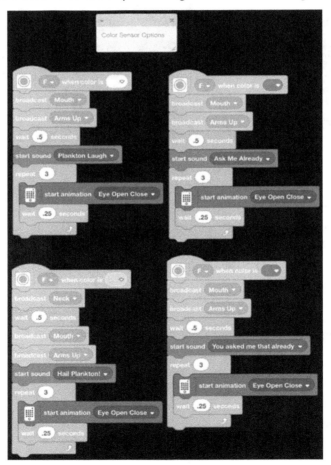

Figure 10.45 – Color sensor code

You now have the color sensor coded, but you now need Plankton to look like it is interacting. To do this, you need to write some code to open and close the mouth when it is talking.

Mouth open code

This section is pretty easy. You will basically write a simple code that moves the mouth motor back and forth. While easy to program, you can spend a great deal of time fine-tuning this to get it just the way you want Plankton to look while talking:

1. Insert a yellow **Event** block named **when I receive** and change the option to **Mouth** in the drop-down menu.

2. Insert an orange **Control** block named **repeat** and set it to 2.

3. Inside the **Repeat** block, add a blue **Motor** block named **motor run for**. Choose motor **C** and have it move counterclockwise for 50 degrees.

4. Inside the **Repeat** block, add another blue **Motor** block named **motor go to shortest path to position**. Choose motor **C** and set the position to 0.

Here is how the code appears when done:

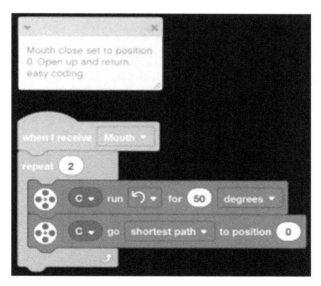

Figure 10.46 – Mouth code

Now that Plankton can give the appearance of speaking, you need to get his arms moving. If you have ever watched SpongeBob SquarePants, then you know he is quite animated despite being a simple Plankton. The key is the arms. Let's bring them to life.

Arms up code

Next, you have some code to write to activate the arms. This is a demo code, so understand that you can change the arm movements *and* you can also create several different arm movement broadcast codes. For example, these arms go up and down, but you could have the arms alternate or only one arm move:

1. Insert a yellow **Events** block named **when I receive** and change the option to **Arms Up**.

2. Insert an orange **Control** block named **repeat** and set it to 2.

3. Inside the **repeat** block, add a pink **Movement** block named **set movement motors** and choose motors **D** and **#**.

4. Inside the **repeat** block, add a pink **Movement** block named **set movement speed to** 20%.

5. Inside the **repeat** block, add a pink **Movement** block named **move straight for** -40 **degrees**.

6. Inside the **repeat** block, add a pink **Movement** block named **set movement speed to** 20%.

7. Inside the **repeat** block, add a pink **Movement** block named **move straight for** 40 **degrees**.

8. Insert the **Motor** block, **Motor D go shortest path**, at position 0.

9. Insert the **Motor** block, **Motor E go shortest path**, at position 0.

Here is what the code should look like when complete:

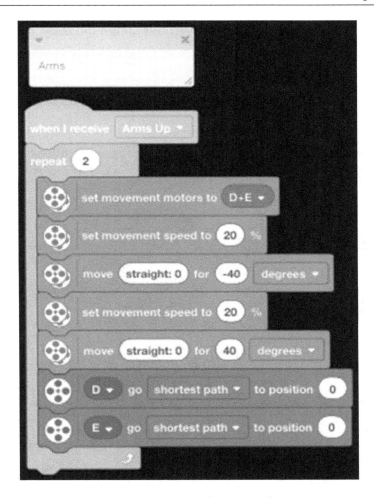

Figure 10.47 – Complete arm code

Plankton now speaks, moves his arms, and looks alive. We now have a few more small sections of code to expand his appearance. The following code section will allow Plankton to move his head back and forth to give one more layer of movement.

Neck turn code

Let's now get the neck moving back and forth. This section of code is just like the previous sections. It is pretty straightforward to code, but realize you can fine-tune and tweak this code to your liking and have some real fun with this code:

1. Insert a yellow **Events** block named **when I receive** and change the option to **Neck**.

2. Insert a blue **Motor** block named **Motor A run clockwise for** 50 **degrees**.

3. Insert an orange **Control** block named **wait** and change to .25 seconds.

4. Insert a blue **Motor** block named **Motor A run counterclockwise for** 100 **degrees**.

5. Insert an orange **Control** block named **wait** and change to .25 seconds.

6. Insert a blue **Motor** block named **Motor A go to shortest path to position** 0.

Here is what the completed code should look like:

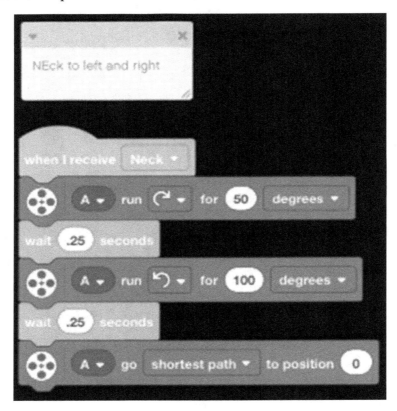

Figure 10.48 – Neck movement code

All the movements are now complete. What you need to add now is sound. You can add sounds from the library in the software or search online and find some files of your own to use. Always practice proper copyright usage.

Random sound generator code

Using the color sensor, you can have Plankton perform a variety of tasks based on color selections. For the demo, each color will have a new sound to be shared, but understand that you can trigger different demands:

1. Insert a yellow **Events** block named **when I receive** and change the option to **Random Sound**.

2. Insert an orange **Control** block named **If**. Within the block, add a green **Operator** block using the = equation. Drag in the name of your variable, **Voice**, and change the number to 1.

3. Insert a purple **Sound** block named **play sound until done**. Add the sound of your choice.

4. Right-click and duplicate this **If** block as many times as you have for colors you want to trigger. For each of these, simply change the number from 1 to 2 to 3 to 4. Change the sound file to the sound effect you want.

Here is what the code looks like:

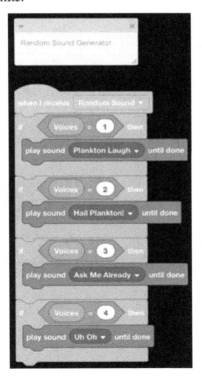

Figure 10.49 – Sound files for bringing Plankton to life

Plankton is now ready. However, you have an additional sensor, so if you want to explore yet another bonus interaction component, you could build another device, creature, or setup to engage the distance sensor.

Optional distance sensor code

The distance sensor is not actually built into Plankton, which is why I made it optional. I created a small little creature that stands next to Plankton to use the sensor. If you want to use the sensor, then here is a sample code that would randomly play a sound file when an object is detected:

1. Insert a yellow **Event** block named **Distance Sensor B when closer than** 8 **cm**.

2. Insert an orange **Variable** block named **set Voices to pick random** 1 **to** 4 by adding a green **Operator** block named **pick random**.

3. Insert a yellow **Event** block named **broadcast Random Sound**.

4. Insert a purple **Light** block named **start animation** and choose your eye animation.

Here is what this code looks like:

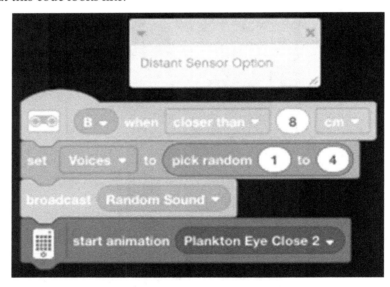

Figure 10.50 – Distance sensor code

Finally, here is the complete view of the code. If this is hard to read, please remember that you have access to the code file to make it easier to view on your device:

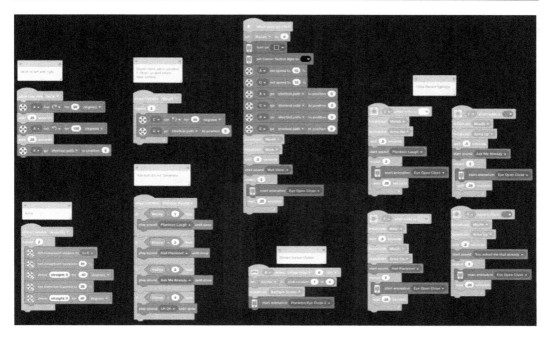

Figure 10.51 – The complete code layout

So now it is time to play and have fun. Enjoy Plankton and bring your own ideas to life.

Making it your own

What can you do to make this build unique to your own needs? Here are some suggestions and I look forward to your creative ideas.

Here are a few ideas to consider:

- What are the different responses that Plankton could have using the color and distance sensors?
- What types of eye animations could you create to bring more emotion to Plankton?
- Could you incorporate the distance sensor into the Plankton build itself?

Summary

In summary, this robot was the biggest build of them all using motors and parts in new and exciting ways. There were many build techniques using gears, attachment techniques, and utilizing the creative constraints of one kit. You used motors to open and close a mouth, turn a neck, and animate arms. You have sensors to bring this robot to life in an animatronic sense, where you can have Plankton interact with his environment and those around him. Finally, it allows for complete freedom for you to make him behave as you wish.

My hope is that this build inspires you to build your own creations, monsters, characters, and suchlike, and that you will go on to do incredible work with all the skills you have gained.

`Packt.com`

Subscribe to our online digital library for full access to over 7,000 books and videos, as well as industry leading tools to help you plan your personal development and advance your career. For more information, please visit our website.

Why subscribe?

- Spend less time learning and more time coding with practical eBooks and Videos from over 4,000 industry professionals

- Improve your learning with Skill Plans built especially for you

- Get a free eBook or video every month

- Fully searchable for easy access to vital information

- Copy and paste, print, and bookmark content

Did you know that Packt offers eBook versions of every book published, with PDF and ePub files available? You can upgrade to the eBook version at `packt.com` and as a print book customer, you are entitled to a discount on the eBook copy. Get in touch with us at `customercare@packtpub.com` for more details.

At `www.packt.com`, you can also read a collection of free technical articles, sign up for a range of free newsletters, and receive exclusive discounts and offers on Packt books and eBooks.

Other Books You May Enjoy

If you enjoyed this book, you may be interested in these other books by Packt:

Learn Robotics Programming – Second Edition

Danny Staple

ISBN: 978-1-83921-786-9

- Leverage the features of the Raspberry Pi OS
- Discover how to configure a Raspberry Pi to build an AI-enabled robot
- Interface motors and sensors with a Raspberry Pi
- Code your robot to develop engaging and intelligent robot behavior
- Explore AI behavior such as speech recognition and visual processing
- Find out how you can control AI robots with a mobile phone over Wi-Fi
- Understand how to choose the right parts and assemble your robot

Hands-on ROS for Robotics Programming

Bernardo Ronquillo

ISBN: 978-1-83855-288-6

- Get to grips with developing environment-aware robots
- Gain insights into how your robots will react in physical environments
- Break down a desired behavior into a chain of robot actions
- Relate data from sensors with context to produce adaptive responses
- Apply reinforcement learning to allow your robot to learn by trial and error
- Implement deep learning to enable your robot to recognize its surroundings

Packt is searching for authors like you

If you're interested in becoming an author for Packt, please visit authors. packtpub.com and apply today. We have worked with thousands of developers and tech professionals, just like you, to help them share their insight with the global tech community. You can make a general application, apply for a specific hot topic that we are recruiting an author for, or submit your own idea.

Leave a review - let other readers know what you think

Please share your thoughts on this book with others by leaving a review on the site that you bought it from. If you purchased the book from Amazon, please leave us an honest review on this book's Amazon page. This is vital so that other potential readers can see and use your unbiased opinion to make purchasing decisions, we can understand what our customers think about our products, and our authors can see your feedback on the title that they have worked with Packt to create. It will only take a few minutes of your time, but is valuable to other potential customers, our authors, and Packt. Thank you!

Index

www.ingramcontent.com/pod-product-compliance
Lightning Source LLC
LaVergne TN
LVHW081328050326
832903LV00024B/1072